CAMBRIDGE TEXTS IN THE
HISTORY OF POLITICAL THOUGHT

———

ERASMUS
The Education of a Christian Prince

CAMBRIDGE TEXTS IN THE
HISTORY OF POLITICAL THOUGHT

Series editors

RAYMOND GEUSS
Reader in Philosophy, University of Cambridge

QUENTIN SKINNER
Regius Professor of Modern History, University of Cambridge

Cambridge Texts in the History of Political Thought is now firmly established as the major student textbook series in political theory. It aims to make available to students all the most important texts in the history of Western political thought, from ancient Greece to the early twentieth century. All the familiar classic texts will be included but the series seeks at the same time to enlarge the conventional canon by incorporating an extensive range of less well-known works, many of them never before available in a modern English edition. Wherever possible, texts are published in complete and unabridged form, and translations are specially commissioned for the series. Each volume contains a critical introduction together with chronologies, biographical sketches, a guide to further reading and any necessary glossaries and textual apparatus. When completed, the series will aim to offer an outline of the entire evolution of Western political thought.

For a list of titles published in the series, please see end of book.

ERASMUS

The Education of a Christian Prince

TRANSLATED BY

NEIL M. CHESHIRE AND MICHAEL J. HEATH

WITH THE

Panegyric for Archduke Philip of Austria

TRANSLATED BY

LISA JARDINE

EDITED BY

LISA JARDINE

Queen Mary and Westfield College, London

CAMBRIDGE
UNIVERSITY PRESS

CAMBRIDGE UNIVERSITY PRESS
Cambridge, New York, Melbourne, Madrid, Cape Town, Singapore, São Paulo

Cambridge University Press
The Edinburgh Building, Cambridge CB2 8RU, UK

Published in the United States of America by Cambridge University Press, New York

www.cambridge.org
Information on this title: www.cambridge.org/9780521588119

First published 1997
Seventh printing 2007

Printed in the United Kingdom at the University Press, Cambridge

A catalogue record for this publication is available from the British Library

Library of Congress Cataloguing in Publication data
Erasmus, Desiderius, d. 1536
[Institutio principis Christiani. English]
The Education of a Christian prince / Erasmus; translated by
Neil M. Cheshire and Michael J. Heath; with the Panegyric for
Archduke Philip of Austria; edited and translated by Lisa Jardine.
p. cm. – (Cambridge texts in the history of political thought)
includes bibliographical references and index.
ISBN 0 521 58216 4 – ISBN 0521 58811 1 (pbk.)
1. Education of princes. 2. Kings and rulers – Duties. 3. Peace.
I. Jardine, Lisa. II. Cheshire, Neil M. III. Heath. Michael J. (Michael John).
IV. Erasmus, Desiderius, d. 1536. Ad illustrissimum principem Philippum. English.
V. Title VI. Series.
JC145.E65 1997
320'.01 – dc20 96–35 84 CIP

ISBN-13 978-0-521-58811-9 paperback

Contents

v

Introduction

Erasmus's *Education of a Christian Prince* and Machiavelli's *Prince* were written within three years of one another (in 1516 and 1513 respectively).[1] In composing their treatises on how best to groom the ruler for effective government, both were responding to the political instability of the times, and the 'moral panic' (as one historian has characterised it) generated by a period of high dynastic aspirations and territorial ambitions on the part of the most powerful princely houses of Europe (the Medici in Italy, the Valois in France, and the Habsburgs in Spain, Germany, and the Low Countries). Reacting to the regaining of power in Florence in 1512 by the Medici family (ousted by the French in 1494), Machiavelli set out to define the qualities of princely virtuosity which will ensure that he can maintain control of the state to which he has laid claim. The precepts he devised to do so, based on the threat of punishment for misdemeanour, a commitment to territorial expansionism, and a readiness to sustain political control by force, are designed to keep the prince's subjects in a constant state of insecurity: 'it is much safer to be feared than loved', for example, or 'a prince should have no other thought or object than war and its laws and discipline'.[2]

---

[1] Machiavelli's *Prince* was not published, however, until 1532.
[2] See Charles B. Schmitt, Quentin Skinner and Eckhard Kessler (eds.), *The Cambridge History of Renaissance Philosophy* (Cambridge: Cambridge University Press, 1988), 430–4; Brian P. Copenhaver and Charles B. Schmitt, *Renaissance Philosophy* (Oxford: Oxford University Press, 1992), 278–84.

It is one of those perennial ironies of human intellectual ingenuity that the responses of the two thinkers to a shared problem in *realpolitik* should have been so strikingly different. In *The Education of a Christian Prince* Erasmus takes precisely the opposite point of view. Whereas Machiavelli set out to instruct the ruler who has seized power on how best to sustain it, Erasmus is candid in his commitment to the hereditary monarchies of Europe, and forthright in his contention that the cost of disturbing the order currently in place, in terms of ensuing discord and social disintegration, is too high to be contemplated. Only outright tyranny justifies political challenge from a ruler's subjects. The problem Erasmus sets himself in *The Education of a Christian Prince*, given this commitment to, and support for, the *status quo*, is how to ensure that those born to rule are educated so as to govern justly and benevolently, and so that the prince's rule never degenerates into oppression.

'A prince simply cannot exist without a state, and in fact the state takes in the prince, rather than the reverse. What makes a prince a great man, except the consent of his subjects?'[3] It is the formal consent of a prince's subjects, according to Erasmus, which entitles him to exercise authority over them. A prince born into an existing hereditary line can assume that consent; a prince who gains his title by marriage must actively seek it, as must the prince who gains a territory through military action and conquest. In each case the prince is expected to make a binding undertaking to act in the best interests of his subjects.

Erasmus's insistence on the necessity of virtuous conduct in all things on the part of the prince follows directly from this consensual model of lawful government. A body of subjects elects to submit to the rule of a prince on the strict understanding that all his actions will be for their communal good. In his dedicatory letter to Prince Charles (later the Habsburg Emperor Charles V) Erasmus proposes (following the Greek political philosopher Xenophon) that 'there is something beyond human nature, something wholly divine, in absolute rule over free and willing subjects'. Free and willing consent both justifies and supports the rule of the Christian prince. It follows that he needs to be educated so as to recognise and pursue

---

[3] ECP, 89 (ASD IV-I, 212).

the morally good in all things, in order to be able to take decisions correctly on behalf of his people.

As a strategic document in political thought, then, *The Education of a Christian Prince* has much more in common with another treatise in political thought published in 1516, Thomas More's *Utopia*,[4] than with Machiavelli's *Prince*. Both authors are prepared to restrict individual freedom in the interests of a stable and orderly commonwealth.[5] Both believe that a state whose dominion is designed on the basis of classically derived, liberal humanist precepts imposed on willing subjects will be fair and benevolent, stable and lasting. This means, however, that individuals are not entitled to object to personally disadvantageous consequences of the social order. Finally, both authors show a marked aversion to violence and to high and arbitrary taxation.[6]

Notoriously, Erasmus was a life-long pacifist, with a deep personal aversion to the kinds of alarming local partisan conflicts in which he found himself repeatedly on the verge of being caught up, as he criss-crossed Europe as a peripatetic author in search of a stable base from which to conduct and disseminate his scholarship. *The Education of a Christian Prince* includes a fervent plea for a 'universal peace' (though he himself argued that the inclusion in the treatise of a section entitled 'On starting war' proved that on occasion he could countenance military action in a just cause).[7] Erasmus's commitment to a social and political environment which supports and nurtures the individual inquiring mind led him unequivocally to advocate peace at any price. Where sectarian beliefs or partisan political commitments interpose barriers— barriers which are at their most extreme at times of actual military hostilities—the individual is necessarily prevented from holding or developing ideas freely and unrestrainedly. In the section entitled 'On starting war', Erasmus argues that a prince 'will never be more hesitant or more circumspect than in starting a war; other actions

---

[4] *Utopia* is available in the Cambridge Texts series (edited by George M. Logan and Robert M. Adams).

[5] See Logan and Adams (eds.), *Utopia*, xii and xxvi.

[6] As Logan and Adams point out, however, More is more inclined than Erasmus to accept war (and some pretty dirty tactics) in the commonwealth's interests (*Utopia*, xxvi).

[7] On Erasmus's pacifism see Ross Dealy, 'The dynamics of Erasmus' thought on war', *Erasmus of Rotterdam Society Yearbook* 4 (1984), 53–67.

have their different advantages, but war always brings about the wreck of everything that is good'.

On the eve of the Reformation, there is something rather poignant about Erasmus's reluctance to regard even intellectual antagonism as other than an impediment to the free development of ideas—an advance indication that in the 1520s he would refuse to acknowledge the part that his own revisions of the New Testament had played in Luther's radical thinking, let alone publicly take sides either for or against the reformer.[8] Or rather, we might consider that Erasmus's clearly stated view that, in the interests of political stability and civic harmony, loyalty to the native-born, established prince takes priority over all other commitments predetermined his attitude to Luther. Once Luther's denunciation of the venery and corruption of the Catholic Church led to civil disturbance and unrest, Erasmus was bound to dissociate himself from the reform movement, in spite of his evident sympathy for some of the criticisms levelled at church practices. In April 1522 Erasmus wrote to Charles V's chaplain:

> Our new pope [Adrian VI], with his scholarly wisdom and wise integrity, and at the same time a spirit in our emperor that seems more than human, encourage me to high hopes that this plague [Lutheranism] may be rooted out in such a way that it may never grow again. This can be done if the roots are cut away from which this plague so often sprouts afresh, one of which is hatred of the

---

[8] The standard view of Erasmus's relationship to the Lutheran Reformation is to be found in E. Rummel's introduction to *The Erasmus Reader* (Toronto: University of Toronto Press, 1990): 'By the mid-twenties suspicions that Erasmus was a Lutheran sympathizer and disseminator of unorthodox views hardened into a general perception. Erasmus became the target of popular witticisms, such as "Erasmus laid the egg that Luther hatched" and "Either Erasmus lutheranizes or Luther erasmianizes." Not surprisingly his works came under investigation by the church. In 1527 the Spanish Inquisitor General convened a conference to examine Erasmus' writings. Although the meetings were adjourned because of an outbreak of the plague, the proceedings were soon public knowledge, and Erasmus felt obliged to defend his orthodoxy in an *apologia*. The prestigious faculty of theology at Paris also reviewed Erasmus' works and condemned a number of passages as scandalous and unorthodox. When their findings were published in 1531, Erasmus was once again obliged to justify his writings. In 1552, after Erasmus' death, the Louvain theologians joined their colleagues at the Sorbonne in condemning passages from Erasmus' writings as erroneous, scandalous, and heretical. Ironically, Erasmus was also set upon by the Protestant camp. Keenly disappointed that he failed to join their cause, they unleashed numerous attacks on Erasmus' (9).

Roman curia (whose greed and tyranny were already past bearing), and along with that, much legislation of purely human origin, which was thought to lay a burden on the liberty of Christian people. All these can be easily cured, without setting the world by the ears, by the emperor's authority and the integrity of the new pope. I myself am nobody, but to the best of my ability I do not, and I will not, fail to do my duty. Only let the emperor in his mercy provide that my salary shall be permanent, and ensure that my reputation is kept in good and sound repair against the spite of certain enemies; I shall see to it that he will not regret making me a councillor.[9]

Here, and in the flood of letters protesting his loyalty to his Emperor's party which Erasmus dispatched during this period, that loyalty is consistently expressed in the terms set out in *The Education of a Christian Prince*: tyranny under previous papal regimes entitled Christians to rebel against unjust rule; under the current, benevolent Pope such rebellion is inadmissible. Charles V's just rule commits his subjects to cleaving to the Catholic Church, whose cause Charles vigorously maintains.

There is one further point of contact between the views expressed by Erasmus in *The Education of a Christian Prince* and his subsequent attitude towards the religious and political ferment produced by Martin Luther and his followers. Before he became Pope, Adrian VI had been tutor to the young Prince Charles—a post which Erasmus himself possibly aspired to in 1504, but which Adrian gained in 1507. In Charles V and Pope Adrian VI, then, Europe had, so far as Erasmus was concerned, the realisation of the hopes expressed in the precepts in his 1516 treatise of 'advice to princes'. Charles V was a Christian prince, raised according to humanistic principles and values under the guidance of the personal tutor who now reigned as God's representative on earth—an Aristotle to Charles's Alexander, or a Xenophon to Charles's Cyrus. To attempt to undermine such a partnership, as Luther was doing, could, for Erasmus, only be construed as illegitimate rebellion and heresy.[10]

The Education of a Christian Prince is presented in the form of a series of precepts or aphorisms (compact, memorable summaries of

[9] CWE 9, 61 [ep. 1273].
[10] On Adrian VI and Erasmus see Allen 1, 380.

the key items of instruction) addressed to the enlightened ruler. Its 'Christianity' is substantially a question of its highly moral attitude to leadership and the rule of law. In the body of the text, the precedents on which Erasmus bases his arguments are drawn evenhandedly from pagan and Christian sources. He ranges widely, with a virtuoso grasp on the political writings of antiquity, and often citing from memory. The tone is magisterial—the youthful prince is encouraged by the humanist teacher's example to immerse himself in the writings of the past (pagan and scriptural) to develop an outlook and habits of thought that will mould him into the virtuous leader of an obedient and grateful people.

Erasmus begins with the characteristics of moderation and a balanced temperament to be looked for when a community sets out to elect its ruler. But he devotes most of the long opening section to precepts for moulding the individual destined to reign by accident of birth into suitable form as a ruler. It is above all else a humane education which makes a good prince. The people may not be able to choose their prince, but they are at least in a position to make sure that he will rule justly by their choice of those who train him for the job: 'Where there is no power to select the prince, the man who is to educate the future prince must be selected with comparable care'; 'To produce a good prince, these and similar seeds should be sown from the start by parents, nurses, and tutor in the boy's young mind; and let him learn them voluntarily and not under compulsion. For this is the way to bring up a prince who is destined to rule over free and willing subjects.'

There follows a substantial section of aphorisms on how to educate the future ruler. Here, as throughout the treatise, Erasmus moves shrewdly between precepts which he proposes ought to be observed in overseeing the education of a young prince in one's charge, and precepts laid down for the mature prince who strives to model himself for right rule. The latter kind of precept consistently presses the prince to regard dominion over a particular territory as an opportunity to serve his people: 'When you assume the office of prince, do not think how much honour is bestowed upon you, but rather how great a burden and how much anxiety you have taken on. Do not consider only the income and revenues, but also the pains you must take; and do not think that you have acquired an opportunity for plunder, but for service.'

Above all, the prince (and those who train the future prince) must avoid the charge of tyranny. To do so he must avoid all acts of aggression, and consistently act for the communal good, rather than for personal gain: 'Whoever wants to bestow on himself the title of prince and wants to escape the hated name of tyrant must win it for himself by benevolent actions and not through fear and threats.' The Christian prince and his people live in a state of mutual indebtedness and mutual service.

This crucial general section of the treatise is followed by a series of sections incorporating more directly pragmatic advice, based on moralising works like Plutarch's essays (some of which were included with the first printed edition of the text). A prince must learn to distinguish between flatterers and friends, since the advice of those around him is indispensable for good government. Flattery of a prince does not just consist of the things said to him by those around him. It extends to statues, paintings and literature produced to honour him, and includes the honorific titles like 'Magnificence' used formally to address him. 'The boy must therefore be instructed in advance to turn those titles which he is forced to hear to his own advantage. When he hears "Father of His Country", let him reflect that no title given to princes more precisely squares with being a good prince than does "Father of His Country"; consequently he must act in such a way that he is seen to be worthy of that title. If he thinks in this way, it will have been a reminder; if not, flattery.'

The next section sets out to teach the prince the skills necessary to preserve peace in his realm. This leads directly on to a section on taxation, since resentment at raising taxes, as Erasmus points out, is a major cause of political instability. Here Erasmus shows his personal prejudice against taxation as such, rather than any grasp of fiscal matters. He reaches the inevitable conclusion that most taxation is unnecesary if the prince will only curb the expense of his personal lifestyle: 'Much the best way . . . of increasing the value of the prince's income . . . is to reduce his outgoing costs, and even in his case the proverb holds good that thrift is a great source of revenue. But if it is unavoidable that some levy be made, and the people's interests demand such action, then let the burden fall on those foreign and imported goods which are not so much necessities of life as luxurious and pleasurable refinements and whose use is confined to the rich.' There follows a brief section on the desirability of the prince's being of a modestly generous temperament.

Like Plato, Erasmus believes that good rule is a combination of a good prince and good laws. The next two sections of *The Education of a Christian Prince* are devoted, therefore, to the proper enactment of legislation under the direction of the prince, and to the choice of magistrates to see them properly upheld. Typically, Erasmus is keen to minimise the amount of interference in subjects' lives, and is primarily concerned that a country's laws should conform with general principles of equity: 'It is best to have as few laws as possible; these should be as just as possible and further the public interest; they should also be as familiar as possible to the people.'

The next two sections are on the making of treaties and the formation of marriage alliances—the two principal methods available to the prince for securing peace and stability with surrounding territories. Except that Erasmus ruefully remarks (on the basis of recent experience in Europe) that marriage alliances are more likely to worsen the lot of a prince's subjects by imposing on them a hereditary prince drawn from foreign stock. There follows a short discussion of the ways in which the prince should conduct his affairs, modestly and without ostentation, in times of peace.

In the closing section of his treatise Erasmus returns to the prince's obligation to uphold peace and to avoid going to war except as a last resort. War always brings misery to a prince's subjects, so that in the interests of his people the prince's main concern should be to avoid it. 'Although the prince will never make any decision hastily, he will never be more hesitant or more circumspect than in starting a war; other actions have their different disadvantages, but war always brings about the wreck of everything that is good, and the tide of war overflows with everything that is worst; what is more, there is no evil that persists so stubbornly.' Where war becomes inevitable, it should be conducted in as limited a way, and as economically and expeditiously as possible. Erasmus refers his readers to the several places—in his *Adages*, the *Panegyric* and his recently completed *Complaint of Peace*—in his own published works where he has expressed his own commitment to pacifism.

The importance for subsequent political thought of Erasmus's *Education of a Christian Prince* lies both in this strong emphasis upon virtuous conduct as the backbone of the polity, and in the continuous influence his strenuously matter-of-fact argument in support of that position has had on political writing down to the present time. His closely argued case for government by consent exerted an important influence on later-sixteenth and early-seventeenth-century treatments of the rights of subjects to resist imposed rule—notably discussions in the Low Countries surrounding legitimate resistance to the imposed Habsburg rule of Philip II, Charles's son and heir. Echoes of Erasmus are to be found, for instance, in the widely read anonymous treatise, *Defence of Liberty against Tyrants* (*Vindiciae, contra Tyrannos*), published in Basel in 1579.[11]

Erasmus was born in Gouda in the Netherlands around 1469, the illegitimate son of a Catholic priest—the uncertainty with which he deliberately surrounded his date of birth allowed Erasmus to fudge the issue of whether his father had actually been in holy orders when he was conceived.[12] On the death of his father, he was placed by his guardian in the Augustinian monastery at Steyn; Erasmus became a priest in 1492. In 1493 he left the monastery to act as secretary to the bishop of Cambrai, who was tipped to become a Cardinal, and was therefore set to travel to Rome. When the bishop failed to gain his appointment Erasmus was allowed to go to Paris to study theology at the university there. He never returned to his monastery, and in 1517 obtained a papal dispensation which allowed him to live in the world as a secular priest.

In 1501 Erasmus returned to the Netherlands in search of patronage, settling in Louvain in 1502. It was there that he got to know Paludanus (Jean Desmarez), through whom he was commissioned to write an oration celebrating the return of Archduke Philip in 1503. Suitable patronage in the Netherlands was not, however, forthcoming, and after a period in Italy Erasmus decided to try his fortunes in England, where the accession of the intellectual and talented Henry VIII in 1509 created expectations of advancement for humanists like himself. In England he became close friends with a circle of Greek and Latin scholars which included Thomas More, John Colet, and Cuthbert Tunstall. His *Praise of Folly* (*Moriae encomium*), published in 1512, was written as a literary compliment

---

[11] For this influential work see G. Garnett (ed.), *Vindiciae, contra Tyrannos, or Concerning the Legitimate Power of a Prince over the People, and of the People over a Prince* (Cambridge: Cambridge University Press, 1994).

[12] For Erasmus's own account of his life (written in 1524) see 'Brief outline of his life', in Rummel, *Erasmus Reader*, 15–20.

to his admired friend More. More responded in kind with the *Utopia*, which Erasmus saw through the press for him at Louvain, and for which he solicited a collection of endorsing prefatory letters from major continental political and intellectual figures, which contributed to the success of More's little satire.

In 1514 Erasmus left England and returned to the Netherlands. In 1515 he settled in Basel where Froben published his enlarged and revised *Adages* and his edition of Saint Jerome's *Letters*. It was in Basel that he wrote the *Education of a Christian Prince*, encouraged by Jean le Sauvage, who was president of the Council of Flanders when they met, but who soon became Grand Chancellor of Burgundy. It was through Sauvage that Erasmus gained his appointment as Councillor to the sixteen-year-old Prince Charles. The appointment was an honorary one, but carried a handsome stipend (which, unfortunately, Charles rarely got around to paying).

Erasmus's revised translation of the New Testament was also published in 1516, and marked the beginning of his religious notoriety in Europe. Erasmus's appointment to Charles required him to reside close to Brussels, and he chose to settle in Louvain (the closest centre of learning). The Faculty of Theology at Louvain was a particularly conservative one, and between 1517 and 1521 Erasmus was obliged to defend his revisions of the New Testament in the face of considerable local hostility (led by the theologian Martin Dorp). Luther used the *Novum instrumentum* as the basis for his criticisms of orthodox Catholic teaching on scripture, and Erasmus found himself associated with the reformers. Naturally cautious and non-confrontational, he soon distanced himself from the Lutheran movement, though he never spoke out convincingly against it. He continued to publish biblical paraphrases, theological commentaries and translations of the Church Fathers. He was condemned by the Catholic orthodoxy, and his works were banned in Spain for much of the sixteenth century.

At the end of 1521, under increasing pressure from the Louvain theologians, Erasmus moved back to more liberally minded Basel, where he remained until 1529. When Basel declared itself Protestant and religious unrest once again ensued, he took refuge in Catholic Freiburg im Breisgau. He returned to Basel (the city he had come to consider his home) when order was restored in 1536, and died there a few months later, on 12 July of that year. Right up to his death he publicly supported the restoration of church unity. The Council of Trent of 1559, however, placed Erasmus in the first category of heretics, and put all his works on the index of prohibited books.

Erasmus's *Education of a Christian Prince* was published by the Froben Press in Basel, in May 1516, and dedicated to Prince Charles on the occasion of his accession to the throne of Aragon.[13] Erasmus had been appointed to Charles's council a few months earlier. He records himself that he presented an inscribed copy to Charles in acknowledgement of the honour; the text is offered as a first piece of intellectual 'counsel', and an act of gratitude and homage.[14] The work went through ten editions in his lifetime, and was translated into a number of vernacular languages.

The title-page to the first edition of *The Education of a Christian Prince* describes it as 'distilled into the most fortifying precepts'— a work designed to instruct and morally sustain the prince to whom it is addressed. But this is not the whole story. The same title-page advertises the fact that the volume contains 'a number of other extremely relevant works'. These include pseudo-Isocrates on kingship, and Plutarch on the importance of philosophers to princes[15]— ancient texts to which Erasmus's *Education of a Christian Prince* owes obvious debts in content and expression.[16] But the most strik-

[13] Charles had succeeded his father as Archduke of Burgundy (ruler of most of the Low Countries) in 1506. He became King of Aragon when his grandfather Ferdinand II died in 1516. Strictly speaking, he did not inherit Castile until his mother Juana's death in 1555 (she had inherited from Isabella in 1504); however, Juana ('the mad') was judged unfit to rule, and relinquished her rights to her son. Effectively, therefore, the occasion for Erasmus's treatise was Charles's accession to the throne of a united Spain. In 1519 he succeeded his grandfather Maximilian as Habsburg emperor (though technically this was an elective office, and Charles had to contest it against other contenders, including the French King François I; on the basis of a huge cash loan from the German Fugger bankers Charles offered financial inducements to enough of the electors to ensure a comfortable victory).

[14] Allen I, 44, cit. Tracy, *Politics*, 52: 'Shortly after his return to Antwerp he was greeted by a letter from Sauvage, dated July 8 . . . Sauvage was conferring on him a canonry in Courtrai "forthwith". Nor would that be all which he might expect "with sure and certain hope from the generosity of his catholic majesty [Prince Charles], my master." Erasmus, not slow to take a hint, was in Brussels by July 10. It was presumably on this occasion that he inscribed a copy of *The Institution of a Christian Prince* for Charles.'

[15] See ASD IV-2, 106–7.

[16] See notes to the text.

ing choice for inclusion is a reprint of Erasmus's panegyric to the Archduke Philip (Philip the Fair), son of Maximilian, on his return to the Low Countries from Spain, a speech written in haste at the request of the Public Orator Jean Desmarez (Paludanus)[17] at the end of 1503, delivered in person by Erasmus, and printed in 1504.

Erasmus scholars have always been inclined to disparage Erasmus's *Panegyric* for Philip as a piece of dismal sycophancy, a hack oration written when the author was looking for patronage and a steady income.[18] Philip certainly gave Erasmus a significant sum as a gift for his pains,[19] and may have offered him a post educating his children (including the three-year-old Prince Charles).[20] In the 1516 edition Erasmus added a phrase to the prefatory letter to the *Panegyric* suggesting that he had declined some significant offer of employment on the occasion of its delivery.[21]

Actually the *Panegyric* sits very appropriately alongside the *Education of a Christian Prince*, particularly if we take into account

[17] Jean Desmarez or Paludanus (died 1525) came from Cassel, near St Omer. As well as holding the office of Public Orator at the University of Louvain, he was a Canon of St Peter's Church. He became chief secretary or Scribe to the University in December 1504. He gave Erasmus hospitality on a number of occasions, and Erasmus always spoke warmly of him. A letter from Paludanus to Peter Gilles and some verses by him were included in the first edition of More's *Utopia*, which was printed in Louvain in 1516, and seen through the press by Erasmus. Paludanus thus provides another link between the 1516 printings of *The Education of a Christian Prince* and *Utopia*.

[18] See, for instance, CWE 27, xvii: 'The problem, as Otto Herding points out in his introduction to the ASD edition, is to know why Erasmus refused to allow the *Panegyricus* to sink into oblivion after Philip's death in 1506.'

[19] 'To a cleric of the order of Saint Augustine, one pound [1 livre] as a gift, which his Excellency gave for his pains and the work he did in composing a beautiful book in praise of his Excellency, touching his voyage to Spain, and which he presented to him on the 9 January 1504' (Allen I, 396).

[20] ' "For already (as I hear) you [sc. Philip] are looking about in order to choose from the entire fatherland some man accomplished in morals and in letters, to whose bosom you may entrust your children, still of tender age, for the purpose of instructing them in those disciplines worthy of a prince." This passage could be read as an advertisement of the author's availability for the position. If there was talk in 1504 of involving Erasmus with the education of Philip's children, it would help account for his later assimilation of the *Panegyric* to the *Institution of a Christian Prince*' (Tracy, *Politics*, 18–19).

[21] Tracy, *Politics*, 18: 'The dedicatory epistle to the *Panegyric* contains a statement to the effect that the archduke, when paying Erasmus for his labours on the oration, "offered much besides if I should wish to join his entourage at court." This phrase was added in 1516 when the *Panegyric* was reissued as a companion piece to the *Institution of a Christian Prince*.'

Erasmus's careful contextualising of the latter treatise in his prefatory letter to that work. Erasmus insists (as he also does in the *Panegyric*) that the prince he addresses—a prince who is Alexander the Great's equal in moral probity and wisdom—already fully exemplifies the precepts he has codified:

> Such is your good nature, your honesty of mind, and your ability, such the upbringing you have had under the most high-minded teachers, and above all so many are the examples which you see around you from among your ancestors, that we all expect with confidence to see Charles one day perform what the world lately looked for from your father Philip [the addressee of the *Panegyric*]; nor would he have disappointed public expectation had not death carried him off before his time. And so, although I knew that your Highness had no need of any man's advice, least of all mine, I had the idea of setting forth the ideal of a perfect prince for the general good, but under your name, so that those who are brought up to rule great empires may learn the principles of government through you and take from you their example.[22]

Charles teaches by example how the precepts of good government laid out in the *Education of a Christian Prince* are to be applied; his father Philip, too, according to Erasmus's *Panegyric*, showed princes throughout the world how to govern well. Thus the precepts in the theoretical treatise are offered as the principles underlying the exemplary rule of two powerful Habsburg princes within whose realm Erasmus himself happens to live.

The *Panegyric* is not the only work reprinted as part of the volume containing the first edition of the *Education of a Christian Prince* which draws attention to the fact that the genre of 'advice to princes' is pragmatically linked to the practical project of finding a generous and committed patron. The volume opens with a translation by Erasmus from Greek into Latin of Isocrates' 'Precepts concerning the administration of the kingdom, addressed to King Nicocles'; and the *Education of a Christian Prince* and *Panegyric* are followed by Erasmus's Latin translation of Plutarch's 'How to distinguish between flatterers and friends', described on the volume's title-page as 'addressed to his Serene Highness, Henry the Eighth, King of England'. This is followed by two further short works by

---

[22] *ECP* 3.

Plutarch: 'Learning is necessary to the prince' (*In principe requiri doctrinam*) and 'With princes one ought especially to discuss philosophically' (*Cum principibus maxime philosophum debere disputare*). This little group of didactic texts, all offering practical advice to a Prince, carries a prefatory letter to Henry VIII, exhorting him to choose his friends with care; and there is also a short letter to Cardinal Wolsey, urging him to advise the English king well.[23] The entire collection of texts concerns the crucial role of men of learning in advising princes. Each dedication emphasises the direct relevance of the texts introduced to the practical business of government in the territories of the particular princes to whom they are addressed.

In consequence, the first appearance in print of Erasmus's *Education of a Christian Prince* clearly and firmly associates the business of the prince's training with actual princes and the pragmatic needs of their regimes. The work is not, in other words, presented as an idealistic, theoretical one, but as a manual for practice. Where Thomas More's reflections on the well-run state in his *Utopia* are carefully distanced from contemporary life and presented in a 'no-place' elsewhere, Erasmus's precepts for princes are strenuously attached to the purpose of the moment—the sustaining of a benevolent regime, for the good of the people, in the Low Countries in particular, under the dominion of Prince Charles, ruler of Burgundy and Castile and (since the death of his grandfather Ferdinand in 1516) occupant of the throne of Aragon.

Nevertheless, one might argue, the exaggeratedly flattering picture which Erasmus paints of Philip the Fair, in a purple prose which often approaches the absurd, is a far cry from the well-tempered and level-headed description of princely rule in the *Education of a Christian Prince*. This is, however, to miss Erasmus's point, that the good prince knows how to ignore flattery, and concentrates on the substance of any discourse directed at him by his councillors. 'It will be no small part of your reputation', writes Erasmus in his dedication to Charles, 'that Charles was a prince to whom a man need not hesitate to offer the picture of a true and upright Christian prince without any flattery, knowing that he would either gladly accept it as an excellent prince already, or wisely

---

[23] All these letters had appeared for the first time with the first printed edition of the latinised Plutarch texts (Froben, 1514).

imitate it as a young man always in search of self-improvement'.[24] Similarly, in his dedication to the *Panegyric*, addressed to Nicholas Ruistre,[25] Erasmus insists that even within the generically flattering form of the panegyric, instruction can be offered on general princely conduct, by attaching the theoretical propositions to the particular example of the prince under discussion:

> My preference for frank speaking made me feel a certain distaste for all this kind of writing, to which Plato's phrase 'the fourth subdivision of flattery' seems especially applicable . . . But there is certainly no other method of correcting princes so effective as giving them an example of a good prince for a model, on the pretext of pronouncing a panegyric, provided that you bestow virtues and remove vices in such a way that it is clear that you are offering encouragement towards the one and deterrence from the other.[26]

The two works together, then, offer two exercises, in two distinct rhetorical modes, demonstrating how a scholarly adviser (Erasmus himself) can usefully instruct young princes in right rule.

Taking the volume in its entirety, therefore, the first publication of the *Education of a Christian Prince* presents a manifesto for the crucial role of a 'philosopher' (or professional educator) in the administration of a properly run state. In 1516 the recipient of the volume, Prince Charles, had effectively already acknowledged such a role for Erasmus, by making him one of his councillors. By reprinting the oration in praise of Charles's father, with its matching insistence on the key role education played in Philip's adminstration of the Low Countries, Erasmus provided an additional public compliment for his new employer. We know that the compliment was taken, from a letter from Charles to Erasmus at the beginning of April 1522, on the occasion of Erasmus's dedicating to him a further work, his paraphrase of Matthew's Gospel:

> We remember for our part how your many distinguished intellectual gifts have been exhibited, partly to his Majesty our father

---

[24] *ECP* 4.
[25] Nicholas Ruistre of Luxemburg (*c*.1442–1509) grew up at the Court of Burgundy and served four Dukes of Burgundy in succession, Philip the Good, Charles the Bold, Maximilian, and Philip the Fair, in senior administrative offices. He became Chancellor of of the University of Louvain in 1487, and Bishop of Arras in 1501.
[26] CWE 27, 7.

of illustrious memory and partly to us. To him you offered your Panegyric, and to us your Institution of a Christian Prince, not only for the enhancement of our name but also to the great profit of posterity. We therefore reckon it part of our royal duty to show you all our gratitude as occasion may offer, for we are given to understand that it is no small part of the felicity of men of genius to find in the prince one who admires their great qualities. In the mean time we will do all we can to promote your religious undertakings and the honourable and valuable enterprise on which you are at present engaged, and will encourage whatever we learn that you have done for the honour of Christ and the salvation of all Christian people.[27]

Here Charles responds to the compliment to his father and himself as Christian princes by taking on precisely the role (support for the 'man of genius' who proffers his allegiance) advocated by Erasmus.

As early as 1517, however, it was clear that Charles did not actually intend to make Erasmus's office more than marginal and honorary. In other words, whilst Charles was happy to claim Erasmus as his humanistic mentor, he would not commit himself to a substantial, regular salary or pension. In 1517, therefore, in his efforts to find a more generous patron, Erasmus made use of the 1516 *Education of a Christian Prince* volume a second time. The episode gives us a clear picture of the political function 'Advice to princes' volumes could perform for their authors—that of literally advertising the author's competences, in the hope of getting him a job as adviser or secretary in the administration of a powerful prince.[28]

In September 1517 Erasmus sent a hand-illuminated copy of the 1516 Froben volume to Henry VIII.[29] Earlier that year he had been cordially received by both Henry and Wolsey on a visit to England—even though the latter was 'a person not generally good-

---

[27] CWE 9, 51–2 [ep. 1270]. It was the confirmation of the relationship of intellectual subject to Christian prince offered by Charles in this letter which presumably triggered the rash of letters Erasmus sent in the following weeks to the emperor's spiritual and secular advisers, reiterating his commitment to Charles, and the Holy Catholic Church whose cause Charles had taken upon himself to support.

[28] In addition to Erasmus's and Macchiavelli's works in the genre, the French scholar Guillaume Budé wrote one in 1519 for the French king François I.

[29] For a full account of this episode see Cecil H. Clough, 'Erasmus and the pursuit of English royal patronage in 1517 and 1518', *Erasmus of Rotterdam Society Yearbook* 1 (1981), 126–40.

natured or complaisant'.[30] According to his own account, Erasmus was led to believe that if he were to settle permanently in England he would receive patronage from the king in the form of a house and a stipend of around £100 a year.[31] When the offer was put in writing by Wolsey, however, the stipend had shrunk to a mere £20. Erasmus continued to negotiate, but the offer apparently eventually came to nothing.[32]

Meanwhile, in August 1517 Henry's Latin secretary Ammonius died, creating a significant vacancy for a scholar in the king's administration.[33] It was at this point that Erasmus sent the specially prepared copy of the *Education of a Christian Prince* to Henry.[34] In a carefully worded letter Erasmus laid out the grounds for selecting this particular work, and discreetly pressed his case for employment. Henry was an unusual king in that in spite of his own exceptional intelligence he still enjoyed 'the familiar conversation of sage and learned men' (just as Plutarch counselled). 'Above all, amidst all the business of the realm and indeed of the whole world, scarcely a day passes in which you do not devote some portion of your time to reading books, enjoying the society of those philosophers of old who flatter least of all men, and of those books especially from whose perusal you will rise more judicious, a better man and a better king.'[35] In other words, Henry's conduct perfectly exemplified the advice for princely rule offered by Isocrates and Plutarch in the items contained in the gift volume.

Erasmus then draws the king's attention to the particular appropriateness for himself of the individual works in the Froben *Education of a Christian Prince* volume. The Plutarch orations reprinted

---

[30] Letter from Erasmus to his friend Willibald Pirckheimer (Allen III, 116–19, ep. 694).

[31] Clough, 'Royal patronage', 130.

[32] For the fact that the offer was never confirmed see the note in CWE 5, 165 (line 11).

[33] Andrew Ammonius of Lucca (c.1478–1517) had come to England from Italy around 1504 in search of a prestigious secretarial appointment. In 1509 he was in Lord Mountjoy's service as a Latin secretary. He became Henry VIII's Latin secretary in 1511, and obtained a number of important rewards for his service (including ecclesiastical preferment, and the office of local tax-collector for papal taxes). He died before he turned forty, of the sweating sickness.

[34] In addition to the illumination, the copy contained an inserted leaf of vellum bearing the arms of Henry VIII. See CWE 5, 110.

[35] CWE 5, 109 [ep. 657].

as part of the volume already carried dedications to Henry and Wolsey, recommending them for their use in counsel. Henry evidently did note and took seriously the directing of these works to his attention: Sir Thomas Elyot subsequently translated them from Latin into English for him, at Henry's request. The panegyric to Philip of Burgundy 'whose memory I know that you hold sacred, seeing that when he was a young man and you a boy, you loved him as a brother, and your excellent father had taken him, not in name alone, as an adopted son', was also (Erasmus suggested) of particular sentimental importance to Henry.[36] The *Education of a Christian Prince* (Erasmus continues) was dedicated to Prince Charles when Erasmus joined the ranks of Charles's advisers: 'I thought it right to answer the call of duty from the outset with this offering, and not so much to tender counsel on this question or on that as to expose in a way the springs of all good counsel to a prince of great natural gifts but still a youth.'[37] As a counsellor to his prince, then, Erasmus represents his role as that of general educator, rather than of providing policy decisions on individual issues.

Since Charles had recently negotiated a significant financial loan from Henry, and was thereby bound in princely obligation to him, it was a propitious moment for Erasmus to offer the English king a 'memorial of two monarchs so very dear to you', which at the same time perfectly exemplified, in its precepts, the liberal regime of Henry himself.[38] Erasmus closes by reminding the English king that 'when I was last in your country, you invited me on such generous terms'—may this gift-volume serve as a reminder (he implies) of those promises of generosity.

Erasmus did not get Ammonius's job as Latin secretary to Henry VIII. The job went instead to Ammonius's assistant, Peter Vannes, who was Wolsey's preferred candidate. Nevertheless, the episode serves as a paradigm for the political possibilities Erasmus understood this volume to offer. A gift of £20 from the king reached

---

[36] CWE 5, 112. On their way to Spain from the Netherlands in January 1506, Philip and his wife Juana were driven on to the English coast in a gale. Henry VII took advantage of the occasion to forge a personal bond with the young Habsburg, and his fifteen-year-old son became close friends with him. On Philip's death, Erasmus wrote a letter of condolence to Henry (Allen ep. 204).

[37] CWE 5, 112.

[38] *Ibid.* On the loan, and the consequent re-alignment of Charles with the English (as opposed to the French) see Clough, 'Royal patronage', 136.

Erasmus in mid-April 1518—a disappointing reward, in Erasmus's terms, but still some indication that Henry had recognised Erasmus's advisory talents as represented in the gift-volume, and might subsequently offer him more secure employment.[39] In the end, however, Erasmus never managed to secure the kind of royal appointment with any of his potential princely patrons that he dreamed of—possibly the terms he demanded were never such as they were prepared to fulfil.

Curiously, it is this tight relationship between an 'Advice to princes' treatise and a bid for employment as just such an adviser which most closely links Erasmus's treatise with that of Machiavelli. Machiavelli's *Prince* was originally dedicated to Giuliano de' Medici, who had assumed power in Florence when the Republic collapsed in 1512.[40] 'It is a frequent custom for those who seek the favour of a prince to make him a present', Machiavelli writes; 'I too would like to commend myself to Your Magnificence with some token of my readiness to serve you.'[41] In the early decades of the sixteenth century, 'advice to princes' manuals were apparently perceived by those who hoped for jobs in the corridors of power as the kind of portfolio of personal accomplishments in the field of political thought which could win them public office.

[39] Clough, 'Royal patronage', 140. When Erasmus replied, thanking Henry profusely for his gift, he also accepted a (somewhat nebulous) 'position' in England, which he promised he would take up within four months.

[40] Giuliano died in 1516, so for the printed edition of *The Prince* Machiavelli wrote a new dedication to Lorenzo de' Medici.

[41] Cited in Harry R. Burke, 'Audience and intention in Machiavelli's The Prince and Erasmus' Education of a Christian Prince', *Erasmus of Rotterdam Society Yearbook* 4 (1984), 84.

Chronology of the life and works of Erasmus

Date	Biographical data	Major published work
c.1469	Erasmus born 27 October	
c.1478–83	Attends school of Brethren of the Common Life at Deventer	
1483–6	Attends school at 's Hertogensbosch	
1486	Enters Augustinian monastery at Steyn	
1492	Ordained priest, 25 April	
1492/3	Secretary to Henry of Bergen, Bishop of Cambrai	
1495–9	Studies theology at Collège de Montaigu in Paris	
1499	First English visit: meets More and Colet	
1500–2	Studies in Paris (visits Orléans and Netherlands)	*Adages* (first version)
1502–4	First stay in Louvain	*Handbook of the Christian Soldier/ Panegyric*
1504–5	Third stay in Paris	
1505–6	Second English visit, staying with More	*Epigrammata* (with More)

1506–9	Travels in Italy, staying with printer Aldus Manutius in Venice, 1507–8	*Adages* (second version)
1509–14	Third stay in England, lectures at Cambridge, 1511–14 (visit Paris, 1511)	*Praise of Folly/De copia/On the Right Method of Study*
1514–16	First visit to Basel; moves to Froben press; visits England, 1515; visits the Netherlands, 1516, appointed councillor to Charles V; supervises printing of More's *Utopia*	*New Testament/ Education of a Christian Prince*
1517	Visits Pieter Gilles in Antwerp; visits England; papal dispensation	*Complaint of Peace*
1517–21	Second stay in Louvain, joins Theology Faculty. Visits Basel, 1518; Calais, 1520 (audience with Henry VIII); Cologne, 1520	*Colloquies* (first version)
1521–9	Moves to Basel, end of 1521	*Paraphrases/On Free Will/Ciceronian/On Writing Letters/ Method of True Theology/Against Barbarians*
1524	Controversy with Luther	
1529	Basel goes Protestant; Erasmus moves to Catholic Freiburg	*On Education for Children*
1535	Returns to Basel Fisher and More executed in England	
1536	Death of Erasmus, 12 July	
1540		*Opera omnia*

Further reading

Erasmus   *Collected Works of Erasmus* (Toronto: University of Toronto
    Press, 1974– in progress)
Augustijn, C.   *Erasmus: His Life, Works and Influence* (Toronto:
    University of Toronto Press, 1992)
Bainton, R. H.   *Erasmus of Christendom* (New York: Scribner, 1969)
Bietenholz, P. G. and T. B. Deutscher (eds.)   *Contemporaries of
    Erasmus: A Biographical Register of the Renaissance and Refor-
    mation*, 3 vols. (Toronto: University of Toronto Press, 1985–7)
Burke, H. R.   'Audience and intention in Machiavelli's The Prince
    and Erasmus' Education of a Christian Prince', *Erasmus of Rotter-
    dam Society Yearbook* 4 (1984), 84–93
Clough, C. H.   'Erasmus and the pursuit of English royal patronage
    in 1517 and 1518', *Erasmus of Rotterdam Society Yearbook* 1
    (1981), 126–40
Copenhaver, B. P. and C. B. Schmitt (eds.)   *Renaissance Philosophy*
    (Oxford: Oxford University Press, 1992)
Ijsewijn, J.   'Humanism in the Low Countries', in *Renaissance Human-
    ism: Foundations, Forms and Legacy*, 3 vols., ed. A. Rabil, Jr
    (Philadelphia: University of Pennsylvania Press, 1988) II, 156–215
Jardine, L.   *Erasmus, Man of Letters: The Construction of Charisma in
    Print* (Princeton: Princeton University Press, 1993)
Logan, G. M. and R. B. Adams (eds.)   *Thomas More: Utopia*, Cam-
    bridge Texts in the History of Political Thought (Cambridge:
    Cambridge University Press, 1989)
McConica, J. K.   *English Humanists and Reformation Politics under
    Henry VIII and Edward VI* (Oxford: Clarendon Press, 1965)

Phillips, M. M. *Erasmus and the Northern Renaissance* (London: English Universities Press, 1949)

The *'Adages' of Erasmus: A Study with Translations* (Cambridge: Cambridge University Press, 1964)

Preserved Smith *A Key to the Colloquies of Erasmus* (Cambridge, Mass.: Harvard University Press, 1927)

Rabil, A., Jr *Renaissance Humanism: Foundations, Forms and Legacy*, 3 vols. (Philadelphia: University of Pennsylvania Press, 1988)

Rummel, E. *The Erasmus Reader* (Toronto: University of Toronto Press, 1990)

Schmitt, C. B., Q. Skinner and E. Kessler (eds.) *The Cambridge History of Renaissance Philosophy* (Cambridge: Cambridge University Press, 1988)

Spitz, L. 'Humanism and the Protestant Reformation', in *Renaissance Humanism: Foundations, Forms and Legacy*, 3 vols., ed. A. Rabil, Jr (Philadelphia: University of Pennsylvania Press, 1988) II, 380–411

Tracy, J. D. *The Politics of Erasmus: A Pacifist Intellectual and his Political Milieu* (Toronto: University of Toronto Press, 1978)

Abbreviations

Allen	*Opus epistolarum Desiderii Erasmi Roterodami*, ed. P. S. Allen, 12 vols. (Oxford, 1906–58)
ASD	*Opera omnia Desiderii Erasmi Roterodami* (Amsterdam, 1969–)
CWE	*Collected Works of Erasmus* (Toronto, 1974–)
ECP	*The Education of a Christian Prince*

The Education of a Christian Prince

Preface

TO THE MOST ILLUSTRIOUS PRINCE CHARLES,
GRANDSON OF THE INVICIBLE EMPEROR MAXIMILIAN,
FROM DESIDERIUS ERASMUS OF ROTTERDAM

Wisdom in itself is a wonderful thing, Charles greatest of princes, and no kind of wisdom is rated more excellent by Aristotle than that which teaches how to be a beneficent prince; for Xenophon in his *Oeconomicus* rightly considers that there is something beyond human nature, something wholly divine, in absolute rule over free and willing subjects.[1] This naturally is the wisdom so much to be

---

[1] *Oeconomicus* 21.12. The ancient Greek author Xenophon's treatise on household management was widely used in the sixteenth century.

desired by princes, the one gift which the young Solomon, highly intelligent as he was, prayed for, despising all else, and wished to have seated continually beside his royal throne. This is that virtuous and beautiful Shunamite, in whose embraces David, wise father of a wise son, took his sole delight. She it is who says in Proverbs: 'By me princes rule and nobles dispense justice.' Whenever kings invite her to their councils and cast out those evil counsellors—ambition, anger, greed, and flattery—the commonwealth flourishes in every way and, knowing that it owes its felicity to the wisdom of its prince, says with well-earned satisfaction: 'All good things together came to me with her.' And so Plato is nowhere more meticulous than in the education of the guardians of his republic, whom he would have surpass all the rest not in riches and jewels and dress and ancestry and retainers, but in wisdom only, maintaining that no commonwealth can be happy unless either philosophers are put at the helm, or those to whose lot the rule happens to have fallen embrace philosophy—not that philosophy, I mean, which argues about elements and primal matter and motion and the infinite, but that which frees the mind from the false opinions of the multitude and from wrong desires and demonstrates the principles of right government by reference to the example set by the eternal powers.[2] Something of the sort must have been, I think, in Homer's mind, when Mercury arms Ulysses against Circe's witchcraft with the herb called moly.[3] And Plutarch has good reason for thinking that no man does the state a greater service than he who equips a prince's mind, which must consider all men's interests, with the highest principles, worthy of a prince; and that no one, on the other hand, brings such appalling disaster upon the affairs of mortal men as he who corrupts the prince's heart with wrongful opinions or desires, just as a man might put deadly poison in the public spring from which all men draw water.[4] A very famous remark of Alexander the Great points usefully in the same direction; he came away from talking with Diogenes the Cynic full of admiration for his lofty philosophic mind, unshakeable, invincible, and superior to all mortal things, and said: 'If I were not Alexander, I should desire to

---

[2] See Plato, *Republic*, 6.503.
[3] See Homer, *Odyssey* 10.302–6.
[4] Plutarch, *Moralia* 778 D.

be Diogenes';[5] in fact, the more severe the storms that must be faced by great power, the more he well might wish for the mind of a Diogenes, which might be equal to the immense burden of events.

But you, noble Prince Charles, are more blessed than Alexander, and will, we hope, surpass him equally in wisdom too. He for his part had seized an immense empire, but not without bloodshed, nor was it destined to endure. You were born to a splendid empire and are destined to inherit one still greater, so that, while he had to expend great efforts on invasion, you will have perhaps to work to ensure that you can voluntarily hand over part of your dominions rather than seize more. You owe it to heaven that your empire came to you without the shedding of blood, and no one suffered for it; your wisdom must now ensure that you preserve it without bloodshed and at peace. And such is your good nature, your honesty of mind, and your ability, such the upbringing you have had under the most high-minded teachers, and above all so many are the examples which you see around you from among your ancestors, that we all expect with confidence to see Charles one day perform what the world lately looked for from your father Philip;[6] nor would he have disappointed public expectation had not death carried him off before his time. And so, although I knew that your Highness had no need of any man's advice, least of all mine, I had the idea of setting forth the ideal of a perfect prince for the general good, but under your name, so that those who are brought up to rule great empires may learn the principles of government through you and take from you their example. This serves a double purpose: under your name this useful work will penetrate everywhere, and by these first fruits I, who am already your servant, can give some kind of witness to my devotion to you.

I have taken Isocrates' work on the principles of government and translated it into Latin, and in competition with him I have added my own, arranged as it were in aphorisms for the reader's convenience, but with considerable differences from what he laid down.[7] For he was a sophist, instructing some petty king or rather

---

[5] Plutarch, *Moralia* 782 A; *Life of Alexander* 14.
[6] Philip the Fair, to whom Erasmus's *Panegyric* was addressed. He had died in 1506.
[7] The original published volume printed Erasmus's translation into Latin of Isocrates' precepts.

tyrant, and both were pagans; I am a theologian addressing a renowned and upright prince, Christians both of us. Were I writing for an older prince, I might perhaps be suspected by some people of adulation or impertinence. As it is, this small book is dedicated to one who, great as are the hopes he inspires, is still very young and recently invested with government,[8] and so has not yet had the opportunity to do very much that in other princes is matter for praise or blame. Consequently, I am free of both suspicions, and cannot be thought to have had any purpose but the common good, which should be the sole aim both of kings and of their friends and servants. Among the countless distinctions which under God your merit will win for you, it will be no small part of your reputation that Charles was a prince to whom a man need not hesitate to offer the picture of a true and upright Christian prince without any flattery, knowing that he would either gladly accept it as an excellent prince already, or wisely imitate it as a young man always in search of self-improvement. Farewell. [Basel, about March 1516]

I The birth and upbringing of a Christian prince

Where it is the practice to select the prince by vote, it is quite inappropriate to have as much regard for ancestry, physical appearance, or height (a very foolish method once used, we read, by some barbarians) as for calmness and equability of temperament and a sober disposition devoid of all rashness: a prince should be neither so excitable that there is a danger that with the sudden access of power he may break out as a tyrant and refuse to accept warning or advice nor, on the other hand, so pliant as to allow himself to be led this way and that by the opinion of anyone and everyone. His experience and age must also be taken into account, for he must be neither so old as to be at risk of senility, nor so immature as to be carried away by his feelings. Some thought should also perhaps be given to his state of health so that a new prince does not have to be found very soon after, which would amount to an imposition on the state.[9]

[8] Charles had been invested with the government of the Netherlands on 5 January 1515.

[9] Here, right at the outset, Erasmus stipulates that the prince not born to rule must be elected by the population as the person best suited to guide the business of the

On board ship, we do not give the helm to the one who has the noblest ancestry of the company, the greatest wealth, or the best looks, but to him who is most skilled in steering, most alert, and most reliable. Similarly, a kingdom is best entrusted to someone who is better endowed than the rest with the qualities of a king: namely wisdom, a sense of justice, personal restraint, foresight, and concern for the public well-being.

Family trees, gold, and jewels are no more relevant to governing a state than they are pertinent to a sea-captain in steering his ship.[10]

The people must look to the same single object in selecting a prince as the prince should in his administration, which is of course the people's well-being regardless of all personal feelings.

The harder it is to alter the person one has chosen the more carefully should the choice be made, lest the rashness of a moment cause long-lasting distress. But when the prince is born to office, not elected, which was the custom among some barbarian peoples in the past (according to Aristotle) and is also the practice almost everywhere in our own times, then the main hope of getting a good prince hangs on his proper education, which should be managed all the more attentively, so that what has been lost with the right to vote is made up for by the care given to his upbringing, Accordingly, the mind of the future prince will have to be filled straight away, from the very cradle (as they say), with healthy thoughts while it is still open and undeveloped. And from then on the seeds of morality must be sown in the virgin soil of his infant soul so that, with age and experience, they may gradually germinate and mature and, once they are set, may be rooted in him throughout his whole life. For nothing makes so deep and indelible a mark as that which is impressed in those first years. And while what we take in at that time is of great importance for us all, it has the very greatest importance for the prince.[11]

state. It follows that fitness to rule will be a matter of temperament and intellectual and moral competence; lineage ('ancestry') is not a criterion.

[10] The ironic tone Erasmus adopts for remarks like this one about the irrelevance of badges of wealth and rank to good government are reminiscent of Thomas More's *Utopia*, which was published in the same year.

[11] Where the prince is born to rule, by hereditary descent (and Erasmus remarks that this is the practice 'almost everywhere in our time'), his fitness to rule depends entirely on his being educated suitably to act in the best interests of his subjects (since they have not actively chosen him as an individual). This education ought logically to start from birth.

Where there is no power to select the prince, the man who is to educate the future prince must be selected with comparable care.

It is a matter for prayer to the gods that the prince may be born of good character; but beyond this it is to some extent within our power to prevent degeneration in one who was born good and to improve by training someone born none too good.

The custom in the old days was to set up statues, arches, and plaques for those who had served the state well. But none are more worthy of such honours than those who have worked hard and conscientiously at the task of properly educating the prince and have paid attention to what would benefit their country rather than to their own personal profit.

A country owes everything to a good prince; but it owes the prince himself to the one whose right counsel has made him what he is.

No other time is so suitable for moulding and improving the prince as when he does not yet understand that he is the prince. This time will therefore have to be carefully employed, so that not only will he be kept away from evil influences for that period but he will also be imbued with some positively good principles.

Since any ordinarily sensible parents take great pains in bringing up a son who is to inherit only a few fields, then how right we are to exercise considerable effort and concern in bringing up one who is being set up, not over a mere cottage but over so many peoples, so many countries, and even over the world, either as a good man, to the great benefit of all, or as an evil one, to their general ruin!

It is a fine and glorious thing to govern well, but it is no less meritorious to ensure that one's successor is not inferior: or rather, the chief responsibility of a good prince is this, to see to it that there cannot be a bad one.[12]

Conduct your own rule as if you were striving to ensure that no successor could be your equal, but all the time prepare your children for their future reign as if to ensure that a better man would indeed succeed you.

There is no finer tribute to an excellent prince than when he bequeaths to the state someone by comparison with whom he him-

[12] One of the duties of the Christian prince is to educate his heir.

6

self seems little better than average, and his glory cannot be more truly illuminated than by being overshadowed in this way.

It is the most deplorable tribute when the succession of an inferior ruler turns his predecessor, who was intolerable while he lived, into someone whose integrity and goodness are sadly missed.

The good and wise prince should always bear in mind, in attending to his children's upbringing, that those who are born to the state must be brought up for the state, and not to suit his own feelings; what is to the public advantage always takes precedence over the private feelings of a parent.

However many statues he may set up and however much he may toil over the constructions he erects, the prince can leave no finer monument to his good qualities than a son who is in every way of the same stock and who recreates his father's excellence in his own excellent actions. He does not die who leaves a living likeness of himself.

For this task, therefore, he should pick out from the whole range of his subjects (or indeed recruit from anywhere else) men of integrity, purity, and dignity; men who have been taught by long practical experience and not just by petty maxims; men whose age will win them respect, whose unblemished lives will earn them obedience, and whose pleasant and friendly manner will bring them affection and good will.[13] This is so that the tender young mind may neither take hurt from the harshness of its teachers and thus begin to hate virtue before he understands it, nor on the other hand degenerate in a way it ought not after being spoiled by a tutor's over-indulgence.

As in all education, so indeed especially in that of the prince,

[13] Erasmus here proposes that the choice of tutor for the heir to a hereditary monarchy is a matter of pre-eminent importance. Erasmus's appointment as a counsellor to Prince Charles shortly before *The Education of a Christian Prince* was published was supposedly in some kind of educational capacity (as Erasmus indicates in the dedicatory letter to Henry VIII attached to his translation of a short work of Plutarch's, printed in the same volume). A passage in the *Panegyric* suggests that Erasmus may have hoped for a job as tutor to Philip's heir in 1504 (Charles was then only three years old): 'For some time (I gather), you have been looking around to select a man tried and tested in personal behaviour and humane learning from amongst your many subjects, to whose loving care you can hand over these still tender nurslings so that he may educate them in those disciplines which are worthy of a prince.' (*Panegyric*, 143.)

moderation is to be exercised in such a way that while the tutor sternly restrains the frivolity of youth nevertheless the friendly manner in which he does so tempers and mollifies the severity of his control.

The future prince's educator must, as Seneca elegantly puts it, be a man who knows how to reprimand without giving way to abuse and how to praise without giving way to flattery; let the prince at once respect him for his disciplined life and like him for his agreeable manner.[14]

Some princes investigate very carefully who should be entrusted with the care of a special horse or bird or hound but think it of no importance to whose care they commit the training of a son, and he is very often put in the hands of the sort of teachers whom no ordinary citizen with a little intelligence would want for his children. But what was the point of begetting a son to govern if you do not take care over training him for government?

The child born to the throne is not to be entrusted to just anyone you please even in the case of his nurses, but to women of blameless character who have been prepared and instructed for the task; nor should he associate with unselected companions, but with boys of good and respectable character who have been brought up and trained in the ways of courtesy and decency. You will have to keep at a distance from his sight and hearing the usual crowd of pleasure-seeking youngsters, drunkards, foul-mouthed people, and especially the flatterers, as long as his moral development is not yet firmly established.[15]

Since for the most part the nature of man inclines towards evil, and furthermore no nature is so blessed at birth that it cannot be corrupted by perverse training, how can you expect anything but evil from a prince who, whatever his nature at birth (and a good lineage does not guarantee a mind as it does a kingdom),[16] is subjected from the very cradle to the most stupid ideas and spends his boyhood among silly women and his youth among whores, degener-

---

[14] See Seneca, *Epistulae morales* ('Moral letters') 52, 'On choosing teachers'.

[15] The pernicious influence of flatterers is also the subject of the minor work by Plutarch, 'On how to distinguish flatterers and friends', printed by Froben with the first edition of Erasmus's *Education of a Christian Prince* in 1516.

[16] This adage could be used as the motto for Erasmus's entire treatise. Given hereditary monarchies, a systematic Christian education is essential.

ate comrades, the most shameless flatterers, buffoons, street-players, drinkers, gamblers, and pleasure-mongers as foolish as they are worthless. In this company he hears nothing, learns nothing, and takes in nothing except pleasure, amusement, pride, arrogance, greed, irascibility, and bullying; and from this schooling he is soon installed at the helm of the kingdom.

Since in all skills the highest are the most difficult, none is finer or more difficult than to rule well; why is it then that for this one skill alone we do not see the need for training but think a birthright is enough?

If as boys they did nothing but play at tyrants, what (I ask you) are they to work at as adults except tyranny?[17]

It is scarcely possible even to hope that all men should be good; but it is not hard to pick out from so many thousands of them one or two who stand out in virtue and wisdom, through whom in a short while a great many others could be made good. In his youth the prince should for quite some time be distrustful of his years, partly because of his inexperience and partly because of his impetuous spirit, and he should beware of tackling anything of great importance except with the advice of wise counsellors, especially that of the older ones, whose company he must cultivate so that the impetuosity of youth may be tempered by respect for his elders.

Let whoever takes on the office of educating a prince reflect time and again on this, that the job he is doing is in no way an ordinary one: it is both by far the greatest and by far the most hazardous of all. And let him first of all approach it in a spirit worthy of the task, considering not how many benefices he can get out of it but in what way he can give back to the country, which is entrusting its hopes to his good faith, a beneficent prince.

Bear in mind, you who are the tutor, how much you owe to your country, which has entrusted to you the consummation of its happiness. It is in your hands whether you prefer to provide your country with someone who will be a benign influence or to visit it with the destruction of a deadly plague.

Therefore the man into whose arms the state has put its son would be wise to take notice in the first place of what inclinations

---

[17] Tyranny—that is, ruthlessly authoritarian rule without the consent of the ruled—is the extreme form of government against which the entire *Education of a Christian Prince* is directed.

the boy already has at the time, because even at this age it is possible to recognise by certain signs whether he is more prone to arrogance and fits of temper, or to ambition and a thirst for fame, or to pleasures of the flesh, gambling, and the pursuit of wealth, or to revenge and war, or to impulsiveness and tyranny. Then at those points where he feels the boy is inclined to go wrong let him especially fortify the young mind with healthy precepts and relevant principles and try to guide its nature, while still responsive, in a different direction. Again, where his nature is found to be rightly disposed, or at any rate to have only such faults as are easily turned to a good use (ambition and prodigality are perhaps examples of this), let him concentrate all the more on these positive qualities and actively cultivate them.

But it is not enough just to hand out the sort of maxims which warn him off evil things and summon him to the good. No, they must be fixed in his mind, pressed in, and rammed home. And they must be kept fresh in the memory in all sorts of ways: sometimes in a moral maxim, sometimes in a parable, sometimes by an analogy, sometimes by a live example, an epigram, or a proverb;[18] they must be carved on rings, painted in pictures, inscribed on prizes, and presented in any other way that a child of his age enjoys, so that they are always before his mind even when he is doing something else.[19]

The examples set by famous men vividly inspire a noble youth's imagination, but the ideas with which it is imbued are of much the greatest importance, for they are the source from which the whole character of his life develops. Consequently, if it is an untutored boy we have in our charge, we must make every effort to have him drink, from the start, from the purest and healthiest sources and to protect him in advance, as if by an antidote, against the poison of what the common people think. But if it turns out that he has already been somewhat contaminated by popular opinions, then we shall have to take the greatest care to release him from them gradually and to implant wholesome ones in place of the diseased ones that have been eradicated. For, as Aristo puts it in Seneca, it is

---

[18] The project of Erasmus's own *Adages* is to assemble as complete as possible a collection of readily memorable maxims for guiding a good life.

[19] Erasmus proposes inscriptions on gift-objects as a good way of making moral advice memorable in another educational treatise, the *De ratione studii* (CWE 24, 671).

fruitless to show a madman how he ought to speak, or go about things, or conduct himself in company and in private, unless you have first rid him of the underlying disease.[20] It is similarly fruitless to give advice on the principles of government without previously setting a prince's mind free from those popular opinions which are at once most widely held and yet most fallacious.

There is no reason for the tutor to withdraw or lose confidence if he happens to encounter a rather wild and intractable spirit in his pupil. For, given that there is no wild animal so fierce and savage that it cannot be controlled by the persistent attention of a trainer, why should he think that any human spirit is so hopelessly crude that it will not respond to painstaking education? Equally, he has no reason to think of letting up if his pupil presents a more fortunate nature. For the richer the soil is by nature, the more readily the ground is invaded and taken over by useless grasses and weeds unless the farmer is on the alert. So it is with a man's character: the more promising, the more noble, the more upright it is, the more it is at the mercy of many shameful vices unless it is nourished by wholesome teachings.

We usually take the most care in reinforcing those shores most severely pounded by the waves. Now there are innumerable things which can distract a prince's mind from its proper course: great good fortune, abundant material wealth, the pleasures of extravagant luxury, freedom to do as he likes, the precedents of famous but foolish rulers, the very tides and tempest of human affairs, and (above all else) flattery disguised as sincerity and frankness. For this reason, the prince must be carefully prepared against all these by the best principles and by taking praiseworthy princes as his models.

Just as someone who poisons the public fountain from which everybody drinks deserves the severest punishment, so someone who implants in a prince's mind perverted ideas, which will eventually be the ruin of a great many people, is the most vicious of men.

Given that anyone who debases the prince's coinage is punished with death, how much more deserving of that punishment is someone who corrupts his mind?

The teacher should make a start on his duties at once so as to sow the seeds of right conduct while the prince's understanding is still sensitive, while his mind is furthest removed from all vices and

---

[20] Seneca, *Epistulae morales* 94.17.

plastic enough to take on any form from the hand that moulds it. Wisdom has its period of infancy, as does piety. The teacher's objective is always the same, but he must use different methods at different times. While his pupil is still a little child, he can introduce into entertaining stories, amusing fables, and clever parables the things he will teach directly when the boy is older.

When the little pupil has enjoyed hearing Aesop's fable of the lion being saved in his turn by the good offices of the mouse, or of the dove protected by the industry of the ant, and when he has had a good laugh, then the teacher should spell it out: the fable applies to the prince, telling him never to look down on anybody but to try assiduously to win over by kindness the heart of even the humblest of the common people, for no one is so weak but that he may at some time be a friend who can help you or an enemy who can harm you, however powerful you may be yourself.

When he has had his fun out of the eagle, queen of the birds, who was almost totally destroyed by that very lowliest of insects the beetle, the teacher should again point out the meaning: not even the most powerful prince can afford to provoke or disregard even the humblest enemy. Often those who can do no harm physically can do so by guile.[21]

When he has learned with pleasure the story of Phaethon, the teacher should show that he represents a prince who seized the reins of government in the headstrong enthusiasm of youth but with no supporting wisdom and brought ruin upon himself and the entire world.

When he has recounted the story of Cyclops, whose eye was put out by Ulysses, the teacher should say in conclusion that the prince who has great physical, but not mental, strength is like Polyphemus.[22]

Who has not been glad to hear about how the bees and ants govern themselves? When the prince's childish mind has digested these tasty morsels, then his tutor should bring out whatever feature

---

[21] In the humanistic programme of education, to which Erasmus subscribed, the child's literary education began with reading (and then imitating) Aesop's *Fables*. Erasmus added an extended treatment of the fable of the eagle and the beetle in the 1515 edition of his Adages: 'Scarabeus aquilam quaerit'. Erasmus, *Adages* III.vii.I.

[22] See Homer, *Odyssey* 9.

is educationally relevant, such as that the king never flies far afield since his wings are too small in proportion to his body, and that he alone has no sting. From this the lesson is drawn that it is the part of a good prince always to confine his activities within the limits of his realm and that clemency should be the quality for which he is particularly praised. The same procedure should be carried on throughout. This treatise is not concerned to provide a long list of examples, but merely to point out the principles and the general direction.

Where the material seems rather harsh, the tutor should smooth and soften it with an agreeable style of speech. The teacher should give his praise in the presence of others, but with sincerity and on valid grounds. His rebukes should be delivered in private and in such a way that the severity of his admonition is toned down by a touch of pleasantness in manner. This should be particularly observed when the prince is a little older.

What must be implanted deeply and before all else in the mind of the prince is the best possible understanding of Christ; he should be constantly absorbing his teachings, gathered together in some convenient form drawn from the original sources themselves, from which the teaching is imbibed not only more purely but also more effectively. Let him become convinced of this, that what Christ teaches applies to no one more than to the prince.[23]

A large section of the masses are swayed by false opinions, just like those people trussed up in Plato's cave, who regarded the empty shadows of things as the things themselves.[24] But it is the role of the good prince not to be impressed by the things that the common people consider of great consequence, but to weigh all things, considering whether they are really good or bad. But nothing is truly bad unless it is bound up with depravity, and nothing really good unless associated with moral worth.

Therefore the tutor should first see that his pupil loves and honours virtue as the most beautiful thing of all, the greatest source of happiness, and especially fitting for a prince, and that he loathes and shrinks from depravity as being the most appalling and wretched of things.

---

[23] It is striking that this is the first mention of Christian, as opposed to pagan, moral instruction.

[24] Plato, *Republic* 7.514–18.

Lest the boy who is destined for the throne should get into the habit of regarding wealth as something of exceptional value, to be gained by fair means or foul, he should learn that true honours are not those commonly acclaimed as such; true honour is the spontaneous consequence of virtue and right action, and he less sought after it is the brighter it shines.

The pleasures of the common people are so far beneath a prince, especially a Christian prince, that they are hardly worthy of mankind at all. Let it be shown that there is another kind of pleasure, which will last, pure and unchanging, all through a man's life.

Teach the young prince that nobility, statues, wax masks, family trees, and all the heraldic pomp which makes the common people swell with girlish pride, are only empty gestures, except in so far as they have been the consequence of honourable acts.

A prince's prestige, his greatness, his regal dignity must not be established and preserved by noisy displays of privileged rank but by wisdom, integrity, and right action.

Death is not to be feared, nor should we bemoan that of others, unless it was a dishonourable death. For the man who has lived the longer is not the most fortunate, but the one whose life had greater merit; length of life should be measured not by the number of years but by the number of right actions. It is not how long he lives, but how well, that bears upon a man's happiness. Surely virtue is its own great reward. A good prince has the obligation of looking to the welfare of his people even at the cost of his own life if need be. But when a prince loses his life in such a cause, he does not really die. All those things the common people hold fast to as a source of pleasure, or respect as excellent, or adopt as useful are to be evaluated by the single criterion of their moral worth. On the other hand, whatever things the common people shrink from as being disagreeable, or despise as lowly, or avoid as pernicious should not be avoided unless they really do have shameful implications.

These principles should be fixed in the mind of the future prince and be engraved on his tender young heart as the most sacred and immutable laws. Let him hear many people being praised for observing these principles and others being rebuked for not doing so, so that he gets used already at that stage to expecting praise as a result of good actions and to detesting the disgrace that comes from what is truly bad.

But at this point some idiot courtier, who is both more stupid and more misguided than any woman ever was, will protest: 'You are making a philosopher for us, not a prince.' 'I am indeed making a prince', I reply, 'although you would prefer a loafer like yourself to a prince. Unless you are a philosopher you cannot be a prince, only a tyrant. There is nothing better than a good prince, but a tyrant is such a bizarre beast that there is nothing as destructive, nothing more hateful to all.

'Do not think that it was an ill-considered thesis of Plato's, praised by the most laudable men, that the state will eventually be blessed if and when either the rulers take up philosophy or the philosophers take over the government.[25] Further, you must realise that "philosopher" does not mean someone who is clever at dialectics or science but someone who rejects illusory appearance and undauntedly seeks out and follows what is true and good. Being a philosopher is in practice the same as being a Christian; only the terminology is different.'[26]

What could be more foolish than to judge the prince by accomplishments like these: dancing gracefully, playing dice expertly, drinking liberally, giving himself airs, plundering the people on a regal scale, and doing all the other things which I am ashamed to mention but which some people are not ashamed to do?

The true prince should avoid the degrading opinions and interests of the common folk to the same extent that the common run of princes are keen to avoid the dress and life-style of the lower classes. The one thing which he should consider degrading, low, and unbecoming to him is to think like the common people, who are never pleased by the best things.

Consider, I beg you, how ridiculous it is to be so much superior to everyone in that you are decked out with jewels, with gold, with the royal purple, with a train of courtiers, with the rest of the physical decorations, wax images, and statues, and with riches that clearly are not your own, and yet as regards real riches of the spirit to be seen to be inferior to many from the very dregs of the people.[27]

---

[25] Plato, *Republic* 5.473 C–D and 6.499 B–C.

[26] Here Erasmus brings together the pagan teaching of Plato, Aristotle, Xenophon, Seneca and others, which maintains that in order to recognise the truth and pursue it the ruler must be a philosopher, and his own Christian princely education, which he regards as also philosophical: 'only the terminology is different'.

[27] Another echo of the disparagement of the material trappings of status in More's *Utopia*.

What else does the prince do, when he displays jewels, gold, the royal purple, and all the rest of his privileged pomp in the eyes of his subjects, except teach them to envy and admire that which gives rise to the filthy sludge of nearly all the crimes that are punishable by the prince's own legislation?

In other people, frugality and a simple way of life can always be maliciously interpreted as due to poverty or to parsimony, but in a prince these same qualities are clear evidence of moderation, since he uses sparingly the unlimited resources which he possesses.

How can it be right for the same man to incite criminality and then punish criminal acts? And would it not be very disgraceful to allow himself to do what he forbids to others?

If you want to show that you are an excellent prince, see that no one outdoes you in the necessary qualities of wisdom, magnanimity, restraint, and integrity. If you want to compete with other princes, do not consider yourself superior to them if you take away part of their realm or rout their troops, but only if you have been less corrupt than they, less greedy, less arrogant, less irascible, and less impulsive.

We can take it as read that the highest nobility is becoming for a prince. Since, however, there are three kinds of nobility—the first derived from virtue and good actions, the second from having experienced the best training, and the third as judged by ancestral portraits and family trees or by wealth—consider how inappropriate it is for a prince to pride himself on this third and lowest sort of nobility, which is so low that it is no sort at all unless it has itself sprung from virtue, to the neglect of that highest sort, which is so far the highest that it alone can strictly speaking be regarded as nobility at all.

If you are eager for the recognition of fame, do not make a display of statues or portraits, for if there is really anything to praise in them, it is due to the artist whose talent and effort they represent; it is far better to create in your character a monument to virtue.[28]

If all else fails, the very trappings of your high rank can serve to remind you of your duty. What does the anointing mean, if not great mildness and civilised restraint on the part of the prince, since cruelty tends to go along with great power? What does the gold signify, except

---

[28] A characteristic response by Erasmus to the flowering of the plastic arts in Europe at the courts of princes.

outstanding wisdom; and what the bright sparkle of the gems, except extraordinary virtues as different as can be from the common run? What does the warm, rich purple mean, if not the essence of love for the state? And why the sceptre, except as a mark of a spirit which grasps hold of justice and is diverted from the right by no tempting distraction? But if someone conspicuously lacks these qualities, then for him these symbols are not decorations but reproaches for his defects.

If all that makes a king is a chain, a sceptre, robes of royal purple, and a train of attendants, what after all is to prevent the actors in a drama who come on the stage decked with all the pomp of state from being regarded as real kings?

Do you want to know what distinguishes a real king from the actor? It is the spirit that is right for a prince: being like a father to the state. It is on this understanding that the people have sworn allegiance to him.[29]

The crown, the sceptre, the royal robes, the chain, and the sword-belt are all tokens or symbols of the good qualities of a good prince; in a bad one they are the stigmata of vice.

The poorer the prince's character is the more alert you must be that he does not become the sort we read about as having been numerous in the past—and would that there were none to be seen today! If you take away their regal ornaments and strip them to the skin, divesting them of the goods they have acquired, you will find nothing left except an expert dice-player, a champion tippler, a ruthless destroyer of decency, a most cunning deceiver, an insatiable plunderer, a man covered with perjury, sacrilege, treachery, and all kinds of crime.

Whenever you think of yourself as a prince, always remember the fact that you are a *Christian* prince! You should be as different from even the noble pagan princes as a Christian is from a pagan.

Do not think, indeed, that the life of a professing Christian is care-free and elegant, unless, of course, you think nothing of the oath which you, along with everyone else, swore at your baptism: that you

---

[29] According to Erasmus, it is only if the people have explicitly sworn allegiance to their prince that he has the right to rule over them. Only if they believe that he will behave towards them 'like a father' (i.e., in their 'family' interests, not his own) will they thus swear. It is the oath of allegiance, not the badges of office, which confers entitlement to rule.

renounce once and for all everything that pleases Satan and displeases Christ. Whatever conflicts with the teachings of the Gospel displeases him.

You share the Christian sacraments with others, and do you refuse to share the teachings too? Having sworn the oath of Christ, will you turn aside to the behaviour of Julius or Alexander the Great? You expect the same reward as the others, yet you think his precepts do not apply to you?

But, on the other hand, do not think that Christ is found in mere ceremonies, that is, in precepts no longer seriously observed, and in the institution of the church. Who is a true Christian? Not just someone who is baptised or confirmed or who goes to mass: rather it is someone who has embraced Christ in the depths of his heart and who expresses this by acting in a Christian spirit.

Guard against such inner thoughts as these: 'Why are you piping me this tune? I am not a mere subject; I am not a priest; I am not a monk.' Think rather in this way: 'I am a Christian and a prince.' It is up to a true Christian to keep well away from all depravity, and it is the province of a prince to surpass all in blameless character and wisdom. You compel your subjects to know and obey your laws; so how much more energetically should you exact from yourself knowledge of and obedience to the laws of Christ who is king over you!

You judge it an infamous crime, for which no punishment can be severe enough, for someone who has sworn allegiance to his king to revolt from him. On what grounds, then, do you exonerate yourself and treat as a laughing matter the innumerable times you have broken the laws of Christ, to whom you yourself swore allegiance in your baptism, with whose cause you identified, and by whose sacraments you are bound and pledged?

If this was all done in earnest, why do we treat it as a game? But if it is only a game, why do we glory in the name of Christ? There is but one death for all, beggars and kings alike. But the judgment after death is not the same for all: none are treated more sternly then than those who were powerful.

Do not think that you have done your duty by Christ well enough if you have sent a fleet against the Turks or built a shrine or a little monastery somewhere.[30] No other achievement will better enable you

---

[30] A comment on the 'token' actions of princes and popes of the period. In 1502 Louis XII of France and the State of Venice had dispatched such an expedition.

to win God's favour than if you show yourself to be a beneficial prince to your people.

Guard against the deceit of flatterers who declare that precepts of this kind do not apply to princes but only to that class which they call ecclesiastics. Admittedly, the prince is not a priest, and therefore does not consecrate the body of Christ; nor is he a bishop, and so he does not preach to the people on the mysteries of Christianity and does not administer the sacraments; he has not made his profession in the order of St Benedict, and therefore does not wear the cowl. But, more than all this, he is a Christian. The order in which he has made his profession is not that of Francis but of Christ himself, and he has received the white robe from him. The prince must strive along with other Christians if he hopes for rewards just as great. You too take your cross, or else Christ will not acknowledge you. 'What then is my cross?' you may ask. I will tell you. So long as you follow what is right, do violence to no one, extort from no one, sell no public office, and are corrupted by no bribes, then, to be sure, your treasury will have far less in it than otherwise. But disregard the impoverishment of the treasury, so long as you are showing a profit in justice. Again, so long as you take pains to consider the interests of the state in every way you will be leading a life of anxiety, depriving your youthful spirit of its pleasures, and wearing yourself down with sleepless nights and work. Forget that, and enjoy your awareness that you are in the right. Similarly, if you choose to tolerate injuries rather than avenge them at great cost to the state, your empire is likely to be reduced to some extent. Put up with it, and consider that you have gained an enormous amount by bringing harm to fewer people than you would otherwise have done. Do your personal feelings as a man (such as anger provoked by insults, love for your wife, hatred of an enemy, shame) urge you to do what is not right and what is not to the advantage of the state? Let your regard for what is honourable win, and let your concern for the public welfare conquer your private emotions. Finally, if you cannot defend your kingdom without violating justice, without much human bloodshed, or without great damage to the cause of religion, then abdicate rather than that, and yield to the realities of the situation. If you cannot look after the possessions of your subjects without danger to your own life, set the safety of the people before your own. But while you are acting in this way, which is that of a true Christian prince, there will probably be those who call you a fool and not a prince at all. Stand fast in your resolve and prefer to be a just man rather than an unjust prince. You can see, that even the greatest kings are not without their crosses if they want to follow the right course at all times, as they should.

With ordinary people, allowances are made for youth and for old age: a mistake is tolerated in the former; leisure and retirement are granted to the latter. But the man who takes on the duties of the prince is not free to be either a young man or an old one, since he is managing everyone's affairs. He cannot make a mistake without a great loss to many people; he cannot let up in his duties without the most terrible disasters.

The ancients said that it is a wretched sort of wisdom which is acquired by experience, because each person reaches it through his own misfortune. This wisdom should therefore be kept well away from the prince, for in so far as it comes too late it has depended upon the whole people suffering great misfortune.

If Africanus was right in saying that 'I didn't think' is not a fit expression for any wise man, how much more unsuited is it to a prince, when it not only costs him dear but costs the state too much as well?[31] A war once started on impulse by a young prince with no military experience may last for twenty years. What a vast tide of misfortune rises from this! Eventually, when it is too late, he comes to his senses and says, 'I didn't think.' Another time, at his own inclination or at some people's insistent request, he appoints public officials who wreck the orderly functioning of the whole state. After a while he sees his mistake and says 'I didn't think.' That sort of wisdom is too expensive for the state, if everything else has to be bought at the same high price.[32]

Hence the prince's mind will be educated in the first instance by established principles and ideas, in such a way that he gains his knowledge from theory and not practice. Beyond this, the practical experience which his youth denies him will be supplied by that of older men.

[31] See Valerius Maximus 7.2.2. Erasmus quotes this saying (from this source) in his *Apophthegms*.
[32] War, which for Erasmus is the ultimate misfortune to befall any state, is regularly represented by him as a direct consequence of thoughtlessness or negligence on the part of the prince.

Do not think you may do anything you please, as foolish women and flatterers are in the habit of twittering to princes. Train yourself in such a way that nothing pleases you which is not permissible, and remember that what is quite in order for private citizens is not necessarily suitable for you. What is a mistake in other people is a crime in the prince.

The more others allow you the less you should permit yourself, and the more others indulge you the more strict you must be with yourself. Even when everyone applauds you, you should be your own severest critic.

Your life is open to view: you cannot hide. The fact is that either you are a good man to the great benefit to all, or a bad one bringing great disaster to all.

As more honours are accorded to you by everyone, so you must strive the harder to see that you are not unworthy of them. Just as no adequate honours or gratitude can ever be shown a good prince, so conversely no punishment is enough for what a bad one deserves.

Just as there is nothing more beneficial in life than a wise and good monarch, so, on the other hand, there can be no greater plague than a foolish or wicked one.

The corruption of an evil prince spreads more quickly and widely than the contagion of any plague. Conversely, there is no other quicker and more effective way of improving public morals than for the prince to lead a blameless life.

The common people imitate nothing with more pleasure than what they see their prince do. Under a gambler, gambling is rife; under a fighter, everyone gets into fights; under a gourmandiser, they wallow in extravagance; under a voluptuary, they become promiscuous; under a cruel man, they bring charges and false accusations against each other. Turn the pages of history and you will always find the morality of an age reflecting the life of its prince.

No comet, no fateful power affects the progress of human affairs in the way that the life of the prince grips and transforms the moral attitudes and character of his subjects.

The diligence and moral standards of the priests and bishops are admittedly an important factor here, but not nearly so much so as are those of princes. Men are more ready to criticise the clergy if they happen to be bad than they are to emulate them when they are good. So it is that monks who really are pious do not stimulate people to follow their example because they seem only to be practising what they preach, whereas if they are not everyone is terribly shocked. But there is no one who does not feel the urge to be like his prince![33]

For this very reason the prince should take special care not to fall into wrongdoing, so as not to turn innumerable people to wrongdoing by his example; and for the same reason he will rather devote himself to setting a good example, so that so many more good people may result.

A beneficent prince, as Plutarch said with all his learning, is a kind of living likeness of God, who is at once good and powerful. His goodness makes him want to help all; his power makes him able to do so.[34]

By contrast, an evil plague of a prince presents the image of the devil, who combines great power with the greatest malevolence. Whatever resources he has he devotes entirely to the destruction of the human race. Was not Nero just this sort of evil spirit in the world? And Caligula, and Heliogabalus?[35] Not only were they plagues to the world during their lives, but even their very memory is open to the general curse of mankind.

When you who are a prince, a Christian prince, hear and read that you are the likeness of God and his vicar, do not swell with pride on this account, but rather let the fact make you all the more concerned to live up to that wonderful archetype of yours; and remember that, though following him is hard, not following him is a sin.

Christian theology attributes three principal qualities to God: total power, total wisdom, total goodness. You should master these three things so far as you can. Power without goodness is unmitigated tyranny, and without wisdom it is destruction, not government. First, therefore, inasmuch as fortune gave you power, make it your business to acquire for yourself the greatest possible store of wisdom so that you, alone of all men, may best be able to see what should be striven for and what should be avoided; and so that,

---

[33] This sequence of thoughts concerning the integral relationship between the conduct of the prince and that of his people also informs the *Panegyric*.

[34] Plutarch, *Moralia* 780 E.

[35] The three Roman Emperors regularly used by Renaissance authors to typify wicked and tyrannical rule.

in the next place, you may try to provide for everyone as far as possible, for that is the province of goodness. Make your power serve you to this end, that you can be of as much assistance as you want to be; indeed, you should want to achieve more than you actually can. On the other hand, the more harm you are able to do, the less you should want to.

God is loved by all good men. Only the wicked fear him, and even then it is the sort of fear which anyone has of getting hurt. In the same way a good prince must be an object of fear to none but the evildoers and criminals, but here again, in such a way that even they retain some hope of leniency, if only they are capable of reform. On the other hand, the Prince of Darkness is loved by none and feared by all, especially by good people, for the wicked are on his side. Likewise a tyrant is greatly hated by every good man, and none are closer to him than the very worst people.[36]

This was clearly seen by St Denis, who divided the world into three hierarchies: what God is in the ranks of heaven the bishop should be in the church and the prince in the state.[37] He is supreme in goodness, and all his goodness flows from him to other men as from a spring. Therefore it would obviously be quite absurd for the greatest proportion of all the state's misfortunes to arise from him who is supposed to be the source of goodness.

The people are unruly by nature, and magistrates are easily corrupted by avarice or ambition. The blameless character of the prince remains, as it were, the sheet-anchor for the ship of the state.[38] If he, too, is overcome by depraved desires and foolish ideas, what last hope is there for that ship?

As God is universally beneficent and does not need the services of anyone or ask for any favours, so it is the part of a prince who is truly great (in that he reflects the image of the Eternal Prince) to earn everyone's good will freely and without regard to compensation or glory.

As God set up a beautiful likeness of himself in the heavens, the sun, so he established among men a tangible and living image of

---

[36] For Erasmus there are no redeeming features to the tyrant—that is, one who rules without consent.

[37] Dionysius the Areopagite, *On the Ecclesiastical Hierarchy*; Erasmus quotes inaccurately from memory.

[38] *Adages* I.i.24: 'Sacram ancoram solvere'.

himself, the king. But nothing is more communal than the sun, which imparts its light to the rest of the heavenly bodies. In the same way the prince must be readily accessible for the needs of his people, and have his own personal light of wisdom in himself, so that even if everyone else is in some respect blind, yet his own vision is never at fault.

Although God is swayed by no emotions, he nevertheless orders the world with the greatest good judgment. Following his example in all his actions, the prince must disregard emotional reactions and use only reason and judgment.

Nothing is higher than God, and similarly the prince should be removed as far as possible from the low concerns and sordid emotions of the common people.

Just as nobody sees God, although he is regulating everything, but only feels him when affected by His kindness, so the prince's native land should not feel his powers except when getting some relief through his wisdom and goodness. The hand of the tyrant, by contrast, is felt nowhere except to the misfortune of all.

When the sun is highest in the zodiac, then its motion is slowest; so in your case, the higher fortune carries you, the more lenient and less severe you should be.

True high-mindedness is displayed not in intolerance of the slightest insult or in resenting any empire greater than your own, but rather in scorning any unprincely action.

All slavery is pitiable and dishonourable, but the most pitiable and dishonourable form of slavery is to be a slave to vice and shameful desires. What is more abject and disgraceful, I ask you, than for him who claims dominion over free men to be himself a slave to lust, anger, greed, ambition, and all the rest of that band of unseemly masters?

Given that among the pagans there were some who preferred to kill themselves rather than preserve their power with great waste of life (that is, who set the welfare of the state above their own lives), would it not be absurd for a Christian prince to be concerned with his pleasures and base desires to the great detriment of the state?

When you assume the office of prince, do not think how much honour is bestowed upon you, but rather how great a burden and how much anxiety you have taken on. Do not consider only the income and revenues, but also the pains you must take; and do not think that you have acquired an opportunity for plunder, but for service.

According to Plato, only someone who has assumed the office unwillingly and not without persuasion is fit to be a ruler.[39] For whoever covets the position of a prince must necessarily either be a fool who does not realise how stressful and dangerous a task it is to carry out a ruler's duties properly; or he must be so wicked a man that he plans to use the royal power for his own benefit, not for that of the state; or so irresponsible a man that he does not think at all about the burden he is taking on. To be fit to rule, a man needs to be at the same time responsible, good, and wise.

Take care not to regard yourself as the more fortunate according as the realm you take over is more extensive. Remember that you are thereby shouldering greater cares and responsibilities and that you are bound to give less and less to your leisures and pleasures.

Only those who dedicate themselves to the state, and not the state to themselves, deserve the title 'prince'. For if someone rules to suit himself and assesses everything by how it affects his own convenience, then it does not matter what titles he bears: in practice he is certainly a tyrant, not a prince. Just as there is no more honourable title than 'prince', so there is no term more detested and cursed on every score than 'tyrant'.

There is the same difference between a prince and a tyrant as there is between a benevolent father and a cruel master. The former is willing to give even his life for his children; the latter thinks of nothing else than his own gain, or conducts his life to suit himself without considering the welfare of his people.

Do not be satisfied with being called 'king' or 'prince', for even those plagues of the earth Phalaris and Dionysius had those titles, but weigh up in your own mind what you are. If Seneca was right in what he said, the difference between a tyrant and a king is in their actions, not in their title.

To put it in a nutshell, Aristotle differentiates in his *Politics* between a prince and a tyrant by the criterion that the latter is concerned for his own interests and the former for the state.[40] No matter what the prince is deliberating about, he always bears in

---

[39] Plato, *Republic* 1.347 D, and 7.520 D–521 B.
[40] Aristotle, *Politics* 3.5.1 and 4.8.3.

mind whether it is to the advantage of all his subjects; a tyrant considers whether it will serve his own purpose. A prince is chiefly concerned with the needs of his subjects, even while engaged in his personal business. On the other hand, if a tyrant does ever do well by his subjects, he turns this very fact to his private benefit all the same.

Those who look out for their people only in so far as it redounds to their personal advantage are treating their subjects on the same level as the common people treat their horses and donkeys. For the latter do indeed take care of their animals, but they measure their attention by the advantage it brings to themselves. But those who despoil people in their greed and torture them with their cruelty or expose them to all sorts of perils to satisfy their ambition are giving free citizens a lower status than the common folk give to the cattle they buy or the gladiator-master gives to the gladiators he owns.

The prince's tutor shall see that a hatred of the very words 'despotism' and 'tyranny' are implanted in the future prince by frequent diatribes against those names which are an abomination to the whole human race—Phalaris, Mezentius, Dionysius of Syracuse, Nero, Caligula, and Domitian, who wanted to be called 'God' and 'Lord'.

On the other hand, any examples of good princes which make a strong contrast with the image of a tyrant should be eagerly put forward with frequent praise and commendation. Then let him paint as it were a picture of each type, king and tyrant, and impress them as far as he can on the mind's eye, so that the prince may be all the more enthusiastic about the one and recoil more sharply from the other.

Let the teacher therefore depict a sort of celestial creature, more like a divinity than a mortal, complete with every single virtue; born for the common good, sent indeed by the powers to alleviate the human condition by looking out for and caring for everyone; to whom nothing is more important or more dear than the state; who has more than a fatherly disposition towards everyone; who holds the life of each individual dearer than his own; who works and strives night and day for nothing else than that conditions should be the best possible for everyone; with whom rewards are ready for all good men and pardon for the wicked if only they will mend their ways, for he wants so much to do well by his people of his own free will that if necessary he would not hesitate to attend to their well-being at great risk to himself; who considers that his own wealth consists in the welfare of his country; who is always on the watch so that everyone else may sleep soundly; who leaves himself no leisure so that his country has the chance to live in peace; who torments himself with constant anxieties so that his subjects may enjoy peace of mind. Let the happiness of the whole people depend upon the moral quality of this one man; let the tutor point this out as the picture of a true prince!

On the other side, let him thrust before his pupil's eyes a terrible, loathsome beast: formed of a dragon, wolf, lion, viper, bear, and similar monsters; having hundreds of eyes all over it, teeth everywhere, fearsome from all angles, and with hooked claws; having a hunger that is never satisfied, fattened on human entrails and intoxicated with human blood; an unsleeping menace to the fortunes and lives of all men, dangerous to everyone especially to the good, a sort of fateful blight on the whole world, which everyone who has the interests of the state at heart curses and hates; intolerable in its monstrousness and yet incapable of being removed without great destruction to the world, because its malevolence is supported by armed forces and wealth. This is the picture of a tyrant, unless something even more hateful can be depicted. Claudius and Caligula were this sort of monster; and so, as represented in the stories of the poets, were Busiris, Pentheus, and Midas. All these names are now objects of hatred to the whole human race.[41]

A tyrant's aim is to follow whatever takes his fancy; a king's, on the other hand, is to follow what is right and honourable. For a tyrant, reward is wealth; to a king, it is the honour which follows from virtue. A tyrant governs by fear, deceit, and evil cunning; a king through wisdom, integrity, and goodwill. The tyrant wields his power for himself; the king for the state. The tyrant guards his security with a gang of foreign attendants and with hired brigands, the king considers himself safe enough in his good will towards his subjects and their good will towards him. Those citizens who are

---

[41] Erasmus adopts a traditional moral educational strategy—that the teacher should rhetorically 'colour' two extreme alternatives, and present one course of action as unequivocally desirable and praiseworthy, while its opposite is abhorrent and to be shunned. He then proceeds to adopt precisely this strategy himself. This passage closely resembles Erasmus's discussion of tyranny in his adage 'Scarabeus aquilam quaerit' (*Adages* III.vii.1).

distinguished for their moral quality, judgment, and prestige are held in suspicion and distrust by the tyrant, whereas the king holds fast to them as his helpers and friends. The tyrant is pleased either with fools on whom he imposes or with wicked men whom he puts to evil use in protecting his tyrannical position or with flatterers from whom he hears what he enjoys hearing. To a king, by contrast, every wise man by whose advice he can be helped is very welcome; the better each man is the more he values him, because he can safely rely on his loyalty; he likes friends who speak frankly, for their companionship improves him. Both kings and tyrants have many hands and many eyes, but these parts are very different. A tyrant acts in such a way as to get the wealth of his subjects in the hands of a few, and those the most wicked people, and to bolster up his own power by diminishing the strength of his subjects; the king considers that his own greatest asset is the wealth of his subjects. The tyrant brings it about that everyone is under his thumb, either in law or through informers; the king delights in the freedom of his people. The tyrant strives to be feared, the king to be loved. The tyrant looks upon nothing with greater suspicion than co-operation between good men and between cities, but this is something in which good princes especially rejoice. Tyrants are happy to stir up party conflicts and disputes between their subjects and carefully feed and foster such animosities as happen to arise, improperly trading on these situations to reinforce their tyranny. But a king has the one interest of fostering harmony among his subjects and of resolving straight away such dissensions as happen to grow up among them—not surprisingly, because he understands that they are a most serious disease in the state. When a tyrant sees that affairs of state are flourishing he stirs up a war, having invented some pretext or even invited an enemy in, so as to reduce thereby the strength of his own people. By contrast, a king does everything and allows everything that will conduce to continuous peace in his country, for he realises that war is the single source of all sorts of misfortunes to the state. The tyrant either sets up laws, constitutions, edicts, treaties, and all things sacred and profane for his own personal protection or else he twists them to that end. The king judges all these things by their value to the state.

Tyranny has very many characteristics and methods of this sort, and Aristotle has expounded them at length in his *Politics*, but he summarises them all under three heads. First, he says, the tyrant is concerned to see that his subjects neither wish nor dare to rise against his tyrannical rule; next, that they do not trust one another; and thirdly, that they have no means of working to change the system.[42] He achieves the first objective by doing everything to prevent his subjects from developing any spirit at all or any wisdom, and by keeping them like slaves and either accustomed to a degraded status or vulnerable to informers or debilitated by self-indulgence. For he knows that noble and confident spirits do not tolerate despotism with good grace. He achieves the second aim by stirring up dissension and mutual hatred among his subjects, so that one accuses the other and he himself meanwhile becomes more powerful as a result of his people's troubles. The third he attains by using every means to reduce the wealth and prestige of any of his subjects, and especially that of the good men; and no sensible person would be inclined to resist him in this, because he would not think there was any hope of success.

A prince should keep as far as possible from all such considerations, indeed he must take his stand poles apart from them, as the saying goes,[43] especially when he is a Christian prince. If Aristotle, who was a pagan and a philosopher too (and not as holy as he was learned even by their standards), painted such a picture, how much more is it necessary for one who is Christ's representative to do so?

The counterparts of king and tyrant can be found even among the dumb animals themselves. The king bee has the largest room, but it is in the centre, as if in the safest place for the king. And indeed he has no work to do, but is the one who supervises the work of the others. If he is lost, the whole swarm disintegrates. Moreover the king has a distinctive appearance, being different from the rest in both the size and the sheen of his body. But this feature, as Seneca said, most reliably distinguishes him from the rest: although bees are very angry creatures, so much so that they leave their stings in the wound, the king alone has no sting.[44] Nature did not want him to be fierce and seek a revenge which would cost him so dear, and she deprived him of a weapon, leaving his anger ineffective. This is an important example for powerful kings.

[42] Aristotle, *Politics* 5.9.8.
[43] *Adages* I.x.45: 'E diametro opposita'.
[44] Seneca, *De clementia* 1.19.3 (paraphrased).

Now if you are looking for what corresponds to the tyrant, think of the lion, the bear, the wolf, or the eagle, who live by mutilation and plundering, and, since they realise that they are vulnerable to the hatred of all and that everyone seeks to ambush them, confine themselves to steep crags or hide away in caves and deserts—except that the tyrant outdoes even these creatures in savagery. Dragon-like snakes, leopards, lions, and the rest of the creatures who are condemned for savage cruelty do at least refrain from attacking their own species and there is safety in similarity of nature among wild animals. But the tyrant, a man, directs his animal ferocity against men and, although a citizen himself, against citizens.

Indeed, even in the Holy Scriptures God has painted a likeness of the despot in these words: 'This will be the power of the king who shall rule over you. He will take your sons and put them in his chariots, and he will make them his horsemen and men to run in front of his chariots; in order to provide himself with tribunes and centurions, with ploughmen for his fields and harvesters for his crops, and with forgers of weapons and builders of chariots. Your daughters also he will make into perfume-makers and cooks and bakers. He will take your fields, too, and your vineyards and your best olive groves, and will give them to his servants. But he will take a tenth of your corn crops and of the produce of your vineyards, and will give it to his eunuchs and his attendants. He will take away also your servants, male and female, and your best young men as well as your donkeys, and will put them to his own use. He will also take a tenth of your herds, and you shall be servants to him. And you will cry out in that day because of the nature of the king you have chosen for yourselves, and the Lord will not hear you.'[45] And let it not disturb anyone that he calls this man a king and not a tyrant, since the title of 'king' was in the past no less hated than that of 'tyrant'. And, seeing that nothing is more beneficial than a good king, why should God in anger have ordered this picture to be put before the people, apparently in order to deter them from looking for a king? He said, in the same vein, that the power of kings was the power of tyrants. Besides, Samuel himself had ruled as a true king, administering the people's affairs for so many years in sanctity and purity. But they, not understanding their good for-

[45] 1 Samuel 8, 11–18.

tune, were demanding a king in the pagan mould, who should rule arrogantly and forcibly. And yet how large a part' is there in this picture of the evils which we have seen within living memory even in some Christian princes, to the great misfortune of the whole world?

Let me give you now a picture of the good prince, which God himself has drawn in the book of Deuteronomy in the following way: 'And when the king has been established, he will not increase the number of his horses, nor will he lead the people back into Egypt with the aid of his numerous horsemen. He will not have several wives who would distract his attention, nor huge quantities of silver and gold. But after he has taken the throne of his kingdom, he will write out for himself another copy of the law in a book, borrowing the original from the priests of the tribe of Levi; and he shall have it with him all the days of his life so as to learn to fear the Lord his God, and to guard his words and ceremonies which have been laid down in the law. And let him not lift his heart in pride over his brothers, nor turn aside to the left hand or the right, so that he and his sons may reign for a long time over Israel.'[46] If a Hebrew king is instructed to learn a body of the law which provided only sketches and images of justice, how much more is it appropriate for a Christian prince to observe and follow the teachings of the Gospel? If God does not want a Jewish king to be elevated above his people, and calls them not servants but brothers, how much less ought a Christian king to do that to Christians, whom Christ himself also calls his brothers even though he is King over all princes?

Now hear how Ezekiel has described the tyrant. 'There are princes in her midst', he says, 'like wolves savaging their prey to the shedding of blood.'[47] Plato calls princes the guardians of the state, in that they are to the nation what sheep dogs are to the flock; but if the sheep dogs turn into wolves, what hope is there then for the flock?[48]

In another place he calls a cruel and rapacious prince a lion, and elsewhere he attacks such shepherds as look after themselves but take no care of the flock, thinking of princes who exercise their

[46] Deuteronomy 17, 16–20.
[47] Ezekiel 22, 27.
[48] Plato, *Republic* 3.416 A–B.

power for their own ends.[49] And Paul said, referring to Nero, 'I was set free from the mouth of a lion.'[50] And see how the wise Solomon depicted the tyrant with almost the same sentiment; he said, 'A wicked prince over a wretched people is a roaring lion and a ravening bear.' And again in another place, 'When the wicked assume princely power, the people groan', as if they had been taken off into slavery. And again elsewhere, 'When the wicked rise up, men hide themselves away.'[51]

What about the passage in Isaiah when the Lord takes offence at the people's misdeeds and threatens them with the words 'I will give them children to be their princes, and girlish weaklings shall rule over them';[52] is he not clearly asserting that no more bitter disaster can overtake a country than to have a foolish and wicked prince?

But why do we persist in this vein, when Christ himself, who is the one Prince and Lord of all, has marked very clearly the distinction between Christian and pagan princes? 'The princes of the gentiles', he says, 'hold sway over them, and those that have power exercise it among them. But it shall not be so among you.'[53] If it is the part of pagan princes to dominate, domination is not the way for a Christian to rule. For what can he mean by 'it shall not be so among you', except that a different practice must obtain among Christians, among whom the office of prince means orderly control, not imperial power, and kingship means helpful supervision, not tyranny?

Nor should the prince soothe himself with the thought, 'These things apply to bishops, not to me.' They do indeed apply to you; if, that is, you are a Christian! If you are not a Christian, they do not apply to you at all. Nor should you be indignant if you have perhaps seen a number of bishops who fall far short of this ideal. Let them look to what they are doing, and do you concentrate on what is right for you. Do not regard yourself as a good prince if, in comparison to others, you appear to be less bad. And do not think that you are allowed to do whatever princes in general do. Disci-

---

[49] Plato, *Republic* 9.588–90.
[50] 2 Timothy 4, 17.
[51] Proverbs 28, 15; 29, 2; 28, 28.
[52] Isaiah 3, 4.
[53] Matthew 20, 25–6.

pline yourself according to the rule of honour, and judge yourself by that; and if there is nobody left for you to outdo, then compete with yourself, since the finest contest of all, and one truly worthy of an invincible prince, is to struggle daily to improve upon oneself.

If the name of despotism is vile, or rather if its aims are, they will not become more honourable by many men having them in common; in so far as moral value is a property of actions themselves, the number of people is irrelevant.

Seneca has wisely written that kings who have the spirit of robbers and pirates should be put in the same class as robbers and pirates. For it is this alone, the spirit, that distinguishes king from tyrant, not his title.[54]

Aristotle tells us in his *Politics* that in some oligarchies it was the custom that those who were about to enter office would swear a set oath along these lines: 'I will persecute the people with hatred and will strive vigorously to make it go ill with them.'[55] But the prince who is about to take up office swears a very different oath to his people, and yet we hear of some who treat their people as if they had sworn according to that barbarian usage that they would in every way be an enemy to the people's affairs.

Obviously it smells of tyranny if whenever things go well for the prince it is worse for the people, and if the good fortune of the one grows out of the other's disaster; as if a head of household were to contrive that he himself become richer and more powerful from the miseries of his family.

Whoever wants to bestow on himself the title of prince and wants to escape the hated name of tyrant must win it for himself by benevolent actions and not through fear and threats. For it means nothing for someone to be called prince by flatterers or by victims of oppression, or to be called father of the country if he has in fact been a tyrant, or even to be worshipped by his own age if posterity disagrees. You can see with how much hatred posterity records the malpractices of once-dreaded kings whom nobody dared to offend with so much as a nod when they were alive, and you see how readily even their very names are detested.

The good prince must have the same attitude towards his subjects as a good paterfamilias has towards his household; for what else is

[54] Seneca, *De beneficiis* 2.18.6.
[55] Aristotle, *Politics* 5.7.19.

a kingdom but a large family, and what is a king but the father of very many people?[56] For he is set above them and yet he is of the same kind: a man ruling men, a free man ruling free men and not wild beasts, as Aristotle rightly put it. Which is indeed what the ancient poets also seem to have had in mind when they accordingly denoted Jupiter, to whom they attributed dominion over the whole world and all the gods (in their way of speaking), with the words 'father of gods and men'. And we who have learned from our teacher Christ similarly call God, who is undoubtedly the Prince over all, by the name of 'Father'.

But what could be more repulsive and accursed than that expression with which Achilles (I think), in Homer, brands the prince who rules for himself and not for his people: 'a king who consumes his subjects'.[57] For he found nothing more offensive to say, for all his anger, against one whom he judged unworthy to rule than that he devoured his own people. And when this same Homer uses the term 'king' out of respect for honour, he usually calls him 'shepherd of the people'. There is a great deal of difference between a pastor and a predator. On what specious grounds, therefore, can people appropriate the title of 'prince' to themselves if they pick out from the mass of their subjects a wicked few who use cunningly chosen pretexts and constantly changing excuses to drain off both the strength and the wealth of the people and then convert it to their own account? Or if they squander corruptly in pleasure-seeking or consume in cruel wars what they have ruthlessly extorted? And anyone who can play the hardened villain in this business is held in high esteem. It is as if the prince were the enemy of his people, not the father, and the prince's best minister the man who most effectively thwarts the well-being of the people.

Just as the paterfamilias thinks that whatever gain comes to any member of the family represents an increase in his own fortunes, so he who is really endowed with a princely spirit thinks of any possessions which his subjects have anywhere as being part of his own wealth; for he has them so devoted and dedicated to himself

---

[56] A fundamental tenet of Erasmus's political thought, and widely adopted in homiletic literature.

[57] Homer, *Iliad* 1.231. Erasmus uses this and the next citation from Homer in the *Panegyric* and in the adage 'Scarabeus aquilam quaerit'.

that they do not shrink from anything, even from laying down their lives, not just their money, for their prince.[58]

It will be worth our while to notice what adjectives Julius Pollux used in designating kings and tyrants to the emperor Commodus, whose childhood tutor he was. For after putting the king next below the gods, as being close to them and very like them, he says this (although Latin cannot translate the words properly because it lacks the special qualities of Greek, I will give the following version all the same so that they may be understood): 'Praise a king in these terms: father, mild, calm, lenient, far-sighted, fair-minded, humane, magnanimous, frank, disdainful of wealth, not at the mercy of his emotions, self-controlled, in command of his pleasures, rational, of keen judgment, perceptive, cautious, giving sound advice, just, restrained, attentive to both sacred and human affairs, stable, resolute, reliable, thinking on a grand scale, of independent mind, hard-working, a man of achievement, concerned for the people he governs, protective, ready to be helpful, slow to take revenge, decisive, constant, immovable, favouring justice, always attentive to what is said about the prince by way of keeping the balance, accessible, congenial in company with others, amiable with those who want to speak to him, charming, open to view, concerned for those subject to his rule, fond of his soldiers, vigorous in waging war but not looking for a fight, peace-loving, a peace-maker, a peace-keeper, fit to improve public morality, one who knows how to be a commander and a prince and to establish beneficial laws, born to deserve good will and having a godlike presence. And there are many qualities besides these which could be described, but for which there are no single words or phrases.' So far we have been expounding the view of Pollux. Now if a pagan teacher designed such a prince for the pagans, how much more saintly should be the plan drawn up for a Christian prince?

Now see what colours he used to depict the tyrant. The sense of the passage is roughly as follows: 'You will castigate an evil prince in this way: despotic, cruel, savage, violent, grasping of what is not his, money-grubber, in Plato's phrase, greedy for wealth, rapacious,

---

[58] Erasmus repeatedly uses this kind of analogy between the father's conduct as head of the family, and the prince's as head of the state.

and as Homer said, consuming his subjects, haughty, proud, unapproachable, bad-tempered, unpleasant to meet, unbending in company, uncongenial to talk to, irritable, frightening, stormy, a slave to his desires, intemperate, unrestrained, tactless, unkind, unjust, thoughtless, unfair, immoral, stupid, shallow, fickle, easily taken in, disagreeable, callous, ruled by his feelings, intolerant of criticism, abusive, warmonger, oppressive, troublesome, intractable, unbearable.'[59]

Since God is very far removed from such a despotic character, it is obviously true that he detests nothing more than a plague of a king; and since no wild beast is more harmful than a tyrant, it is indisputable that nothing is more detestable to humanity in general than an evil prince. But who would even wish to live hated and cursed by God and man alike? Thus, when Octavius Augustus realised that there were continual conspiracies against his life, so that when one was put down another followed in its wake, he did not think his life worth so much that he should preserve his own safety at the cost of so much bloodshed among the people, since everyone hated him.

So also a realm governed honourably and benevolently is not only more peaceful and pleasant but also more stable and long-lasting; this can easily be seen from ancient history. No tyrant was so well defended that he stayed in power very long, and whenever a state's government degenerated into tyranny this clearly hastened its downfall.

He who is feared by all must himself be in fear of many, and he whom the majority of people want dead cannot be safe.

In the past the honours of divinity were accorded to those who had governed well; but there was a law about tyrants, which nowadays applies to wolves and bears, that a reward would be paid from public funds for doing away with a public enemy.

In early times, kings were appointed, by popular agreement, simply because of their exceptional qualities, which were called heroic to suggest that they were more than human and approaching the divine. Let princes therefore remember their origins, in the realisation that they are not princes at all if they lack what it was that made princes in the first place.

[59] Julius Pollux, *Onomasticon* 1.40–2. In Erasmus's text both these quotations are given first in Greek, and then rendered in Latin.

Although there are many kinds of state, it is pretty well agreed among the philosophers that the most healthy form is monarchy; not surprisingly, for, by analogy with the deity, when the totality of things is in one person's power, then indeed, in so far as he is in this respect in the image of God, he excels everyone else in wisdom and goodness, and, being quite independent, concentrates exclusively on helping the state. Anything different from this would have to be the worst type of state, since it would be in conflict with that which is the best.

If it happens that your prince is complete with all the virtues, then monarchy pure and simple is the thing. But since this would probably never happen, although it is a fine ideal to entertain, if no more than an ordinary man is presented (things being what they are nowadays), then monarchy should preferably be checked and diluted with a mixture of aristocracy and democracy to prevent it ever breaking out into tyranny; and just as the elements mutually balance each other, so let the state be stabilised with a similar control. For if the prince is well disposed to the state, he will conclude that under such a system his power is not restricted but sustained. But if he is not, it is all the more necessary as something to blunt and break the violence of one man.

Although there are many kinds of authority (man over animals, master over slaves, father over children, husband over wife), Aristotle pronounces a king's authority to be the finest of all and calls it particularly godlike in that it seems to have something more than mortal about it.[60] If then it is godlike to rule as a king, it follows that to be a tyrant must be to play the part of him who is the opposite of God.

One slave is preferable to another, as the proverb puts it, just as one master is more powerful than another, one art more distinguished than another art, or one service better than another. But the prince must excel in the best kind of wisdom, namely, an understanding of how to administer the state justly.

It is a master's job to give orders, a servant's to obey them. A tyrant gives what orders he pleases, a prince what he has judged to be best for the state. What sort of orders, then, will someone give who does not know what is best? Or even someone who mistakes the

[60] Aristotle, *Politics* 4.2.2.

37

worst for the best when blinded either by ignorance or by emotion?

Just as it is the job of the eyes to see, of the ears to hear, and of the nostrils to smell, so it is the prince's job to look to the people's interests. But wisdom is the only means by which he can look to those interests, so that if a prince lacks it he will no more look to the state's interests than a blind eye will see.

In his *Oeconomicus*, Xenophon writes that it is somewhat godlike, rather than human, to rule over free men with their consent.[61] For ruling over dumb animals or people forcibly enslaved is menial. But man is a godlike animal, and free twice over: once by nature, and again by his laws. In the same way, it is a sign of the highest and clearly godlike virtue for a king so to moderate his rule that the people feel it as a benefaction and not as enslavement.

Beware of regarding as your own only those people whose efforts you make use of in your kitchens, on your hunts, or in domestic services, since very often no people are less yours; but think of the whole range of your subjects as belonging equally to you. And if anyone is to be picked out from them all, be sure to have as your closest and most intimate associate such a man as is of the highest character and who has the greatest love for the country and for the state. When you visit your cities, do not think to yourself like this: 'I am the master of all these; they are at my disposal; I can do what I like with them.' But if you want to think about it as a good prince should, do so along these lines: 'Everything here has been put in my trust, and I must therefore keep a good watch over it so that I may hand it back in better condition than I received it.'

When you survey the countless multitude of your subjects, beware of thinking: 'These many servants I have.' Think rather: 'So many thousands of people depend on my watchfulness; to me alone they have entrusted themselves and their property for protection; they look upon me as a parent, I can be of help to so many thousands if I establish myself as a good prince over them, but if as an evil one I can harm even more. Must I not therefore take the greatest pains not to be wicked, and not to harm so many human beings?'

Always bear in mind that the words 'dominion', 'imperial authority', 'kingdom', 'majesty', and 'power' are pagan terms, not

[61] Xenophon, *Oeconomicus* 21.12.

Christian, the 'imperial authority' of Christians is nothing other than administration, benefaction, and guardianship.[62]

But if these words are still to your liking, be sure to remember how the pagan philosophers themselves understood and expounded them: that the prince's authority over a people is the same as that of the mind over the body. The mind has control over the body because it is wiser than the body, but its control is exercised for the great advantage of the body rather than for its own, and the happiness of the body consists in the rule of the mind.

What the heart is in the living body the prince is in the state. Since it is the fount of the blood and of the spirits, it imparts life to the whole body, but if it is impaired, it debilitates every part of the body. Just as that organ in the living body is the last one of all to be affected by disease and is thought to retain the last vestiges of life, so the prince ought to remain quite uncontaminated by any taint of foolishness if that sort of condition overtakes his people.[63]

As in man the most important part, which is of course the mind, is in control, and within the mind in turn the highest part, namely reason, presides, and what rules over the whole creation is the highest of all, namely God, just so whoever has, as it were, taken over the ruling part in the great body of the state must surpass the rest in integrity, wisdom, and watchfulness. And the prince must be as much superior in these qualities to his officials as they are to the common people.

If there is any evil in the mind, it arises from being in contact with the body, which is at the mercy of the emotions; and whatever good the body has springs from the mind as from a fountain. And just as it would be paradoxical and contrary to nature if harmful influences were to spread from the mind into the body and if the well-being of the body were vitiated by disease of the mind, so it would be utterly grotesque if wars, insurrections, corrupt behaviour, immoral legislation, corrupt officials, and other plagues of this kind upon the state were to proceed from princes themselves, when it is their wisdom which should have composed such unrest as arises

---

[62] Erasmus is here treading a thin line between moral instruction and political comment, since all these terms were associated with the rule of the Habsburg emperor, Maximilian, whose empire Charles would take over in 1519.

[63] Another crucial set of analogies for Erasmus, in which the prince is the heart within the organic body of the body politic.

from the foolishness of the common people. But we very often see flourishing states, which have been well established by the efforts of the people, overthrown by the malpractice of their princes.[64]

How unchristian it is to rejoice in the title of 'master' when quite a few rulers who were foreign to Christ have shunned it and have refused, through fear of resentment, to be called what they actually wanted, in their ambition, to be. But will the same Christian prince think it right for himself to be styled 'Magnificent'?[65]

Despite having usurped imperial office by criminal acts, Octavius Augustus thought it offensive to be called 'master'; and when an actor used that style in front of all the people, his facial expression and his comments disclaimed it as if it were a term of reproach for tyrants. And will not a Christian prince display the same humility as the pagan?

If you are the master of all your people, it follows that they must be your slaves; in which case you must look out lest, in line with the old proverb, in every slave you may have an enemy.

Since nature created all men free and slavery was imposed upon nature (a fact which even the laws of the pagans concede), consider how inappropriate it is for a Christian to acquire mastery over fellow-Christians, whom the laws did not intend to be slaves and whom Christ redeemed from all slavery. Paul is a witness to this when he calls Onesimus, who had been born a slave, the brother of his former master Philemon once he had been baptised.[66]

What a mockery it is to regard as slaves those whom Christ redeemed with the same blood as redeemed you, whom he set free into the same freedom as you, and whom he has called to inherit immortality along with you, and to impose the yoke of slavery on those who have the same Lord and Prince as you do in Jesus Christ! Since Christians have only one Lord, why do those who carry out his functions prefer to take their pattern of government from anyone but him who alone is to be emulated in all things? It is quite proper to take over from others anything of virtue that they happen to have in their make-up, but in him is the perfect model of all

[64] Within Erasmus's extended analogy of the state as body politic, warfare and insurrection are typically diseases and disintegrations of the body.

[65] 'Magnificent' was a title adopted by a number of European princes, including, of course, Lorenzo the Magnificent, of the Medici family in Florence.

[66] Colossians 4, 9.

virtue and wisdom. This does indeed seem a foolish idea, but only to unbelievers: for us, if we are true believers, he is the goodness of God and the wisdom of God.

I would not want you to think to yourself at this point, 'But that is serving, not ruling.' Far from it: it is the finest kind of ruling—unless perhaps you regard God as a servant because he has no recompense for regulating this universe, in which everything experiences his good will and no reward is paid to him; unless the mind appears to be a servant because it is so assiduous in looking after the body's well-being even though it has no need of it; unless the eye is thought to be the servant of the other parts of the body because it is on the watch for them all.

You could well look at it in this way: if, by practising Circe's art, someone were to turn all the people you call your subjects into pigs and donkeys, would you not say that your empire had been devalued? I think you would. And yet you can have more control over pigs and donkeys than you can over men, for you can drive them where you please or divide them up or even slaughter them. Consequently he who turns free citizens into slaves will have devalued his empire. The more prestigious that which is subject to your rule is, the more magnificent and glorious is your reign. Therefore he who protects the freedom and dignity of the subjects contributes to your regal grandeur.

To avoid ruling over subjects who are under duress, God himself bestowed free will upon both angels and men so as to make his power more splendid and majestic. And what man thinks highly of himself on the ground that he rules a people kept down by fear like a herd of cattle?

Do not let it escape you that what is said in the Gospels or in the apostolic writings about the need to endure masters, obey officials, do honour to the king, and pay taxes is to be taken as referring to pagan princes, since at that time there were not yet any Christian princes. The instruction is for non-Christian authorities to be obeyed lest any disturbance of the civil order should occur, provided only that they keep within their jurisdiction and do not give orders that offend God. A pagan prince requires to be honoured; Paul says honour is to be shown him. He levies a tax; Paul wants the tax to be paid. He exacts tribute; Paul instructs them to pay the tribute. For the Christian man is in no way diminished by these things, and these rulers do have some sort of rightful power and should not be provoked whenever occasion arises. But what does he go on to say about Christians? 'You ought not', he says, 'to have any debts among yourselves, except to love one another.' Otherwise we should have to say that Christ really owed tribute to Caesar, just because it is on record that he paid up a didrachma.[67]

In the Gospel, when he was schemingly asked whether a people which thought itself dedicated to God should pay dues to Caesar he asked for a coin to be shown him; and when it was shown he gave no sign of recognising it but inquired, as if he did not know, whose image and legend it bore. When the answer came that they were Caesar's, he replied equivocally to those who were trying to catch him out: 'Give to Caesar the things that are Caesar's, and to God those that are God's.'[68] Thus he at once evaded the questioner's trap and also took the opportunity of exhorting devotion to God to whom we owe everything. Moreover, it was as if to say: 'It is up to you to look to what you owe to Caesar, whom I have nothing to do with; consider rather what you owe to God, whose work (and not Caesar's) I am carrying out.'

I hope that on this point such thoughts as these will not occur to anyone: 'Why then do you take away the prince's own rights and attribute more to the pagan than to the Christian?' But I do not; I stand up for the rights of the Christian prince. It is the right of a pagan prince to oppress his people by fear, to compel them to do humiliating tasks, to dispossess them, to plunder their goods and finally make martyrs of them: that is a pagan prince's right. You do not want the Christian prince to have the same, do you? Or will his rightful power seem to be reduced if these things are denied him?

Authority is not lost to him who rules in a Christian way; but he maintains it in other ways, and indeed much more gloriously and more securely. You will be able to grasp that this is so from the following considerations. First, people you oppress with servitude are not really yours because it takes general agreement to make a prince. But in the end those are truly yours who obey you voluntarily and of their own accord. Next, when your subjects are compelled through fear, you do not possess even the half of them: their

[67] Romans 13, 1–8.
[68] Matthew 22, 16–22.

42

bodies are in your power, but their spirit is estranged from you. But when Christian charity binds prince and people together, then everything is yours whenever occasion demands. For the good prince does not make demands except when the country's interests demand it. Again, when there is domination and not good will, however much the prince exacts, he inevitably has less than when everything is his. He acquires most who requires nothing, but commands respect.

Moreover, the honour shown to the tyrant is not honour at all, but flattery or pretence; it is not obedience, but servitude; nor is the magnificence he displays genuine, but rather arrogance; he possesses not authority, but force. But he who acts as a Christian prince has all these things in their true form. He who does not demand respect receives more respect than anyone else; no one is more willingly obeyed than he who does not require obedience; for nobody do people pour out their wealth more readily than for him who they think will devote it to the public advantage and return it with interest.

There is a mutual interchange between the prince and the people. The people owe you their tribute, they owe you obedience and respect; but you in turn owe the people a good and vigilant prince. When you exact a tax, which is as it were owed by your people, be sure that you first put yourself to the test as to whether you have discharged the obligation of your office to them.

Aristotle says that the essence of mastery consists not in possessing slaves but rather in using them.[69] But nevertheless the office of prince depends much less upon titles and statues and the collection of revenue than upon taking thought for the people.

Since the state is a kind of body composed of different parts, among whose number is the prince himself (even if he is exceptional), it will be important to maintain a balance that is for the good of them all, and does not result in one or other becoming plump and vigorous while the rest are weakened. For if the prince rejoices and prospers in the misfortunes of the state, he is neither a part of the state nor a prince, but a robber.

Aristotle put forward the idea that a slave is a living part of his master, if indeed he is a true master.[70] There is at least both a

[69] Aristotle, *Politics* 1.2.23.
[70] Aristotle, *Politics* 1.2.20.

friendly relationship between the part and the whole and some advantage to each from the other. If this is true between an owner and a slave bought under the hammer, as they say, how much more should it be so between a Christian populace and a Christian prince?[71]

If a prince's thoughts and actions are concerned exclusively with extorting as much money as possible from the people, with gathering in the greatest possible revenue by his laws, and with selling magistracies and government offices to the highest bidder, then, I ask you, should he be called a prince rather than a merchant, or, as I would more accurately call him, a robber?

When Croesus, after the capture of his city, saw the soldiers of Cyrus rushing about with a great tumult, he asked what they were doing. When Cyrus replied that they were doing what a victorious army usually does, plundering the people's goods, he said to him: 'What is this I hear? Are not these things already yours, since you have conquered me? So why do your men plunder your own things?' Cyrus took the point, and restrained his soldiers from their looting.[72] The prince should always bear that same point in mind: these things which are being extorted are mine, these people who are being deprived and oppressed are mine, and what wrongs I do to them I do to myself.

Be sure to govern in such a way that you can easily give a justification for what you have done; and if nobody requires it, you are all the more obliged to require it of yourself. For the time will come, and that quite soon, when justification will be required of you by him to whom it will make no difference that you have been a prince, except that the greater the power that was entrusted to you, the stricter will be the judge with whom you are faced. Even if you alone are monarch of the whole world, this is a judge whom you will not be able to deceive or escape or intimidate or corrupt.

When once you have dedicated yourself to the state, you are no longer at liberty to live in your own way: you must maintain and cultivate the role you have undertaken.

---

[71] Where Erasmus cites an argument from Aristotle's *Politics*, he tends to go on to argue that if this is so for Aristotle, how much the more ought it to be so in the case of a Christian prince.

[72] Herodotus I.88.

44

Nobody enters an Olympic contest without first weighing up what the rules of that contest require. And he does not complain that the sun disturbs him or the dust or the sweat or anything else of this kind, because all these things are part and parcel of the very conditions of the event. In the same way, someone who undertakes to govern must first weigh up in his mind what the demands of the prince's office are. He must take account of the other people's interests and disregard his own; he must keep watch so that others are allowed to sleep; he must work so that others may take their leisure. He must show the highest integrity of character, although in others ordinary decency suffices. His mind must be drained of all personal feeling, and while he is engaged in public business he must think of nothing but the people. He must do good even to those who are ungrateful, even to those who do not understand, and even to those who resist him. If these things are not to your liking, why do you enter the office of government? Or why do you not give up to someone else what chance handed down to you? And if this is not possible, do at least delegate any executive authority to someone who has the qualities which you should have shown yourself.[73]

It was very wisely said by one of the wise Greeks that what is excellent is also difficult.[74] Consequently it must be remembered that to prove oneself a good prince is indeed by far the finest thing of all, but is at the same time much the most difficult of all. Nor must you be at all disturbed if at the present time you see some princes living in such a way as to make it seem that being the father of a family is harder than being a prince, and that there is some sense in the old proverb which says kings and fools are born, not made.[75]

Therefore since all other men take pains to study in advance the skill which they aim to profess, how much more attentively ought the prince to learn beforehand about the principles of government? And indeed attainment in the other skills depends mainly upon four factors: natural aptitude, instruction, demonstration, and practice.

---

[73] A characteristic comparison in which Erasmus implies rhetorically that the office of prince requires that unless a man be in peak condition, drilled and trained to the utmost, it is a nonsense for him to aspire to rule a state.

[74] *Adages* II.i.12. See Plutarch, *Moralia* 6 C, and Plato, *Republic* 4.435 C and 6.497 D.

[75] *Adages* I.iii.1.

Plato looks for a smooth and tranquil temperament in the prince. For while he admits that lively and excitable people are suitable for training, he denies that they are appropriate for administering the state.[76] There are some temperamental defects which can be remedied by upbringing and special attention, but one can come up against a nature which is either so brainless or so wild and truculent that to try to train it would be a waste of effort. Nero's nature was so corrupt that even that saintly teacher Seneca could not prevent his becoming a most pestilential ruler.

Instruction must be implanted, as I have said, from the start, and it must be worthy of a true prince, and unambiguous; which is why Plato wanted his guardians to come to dialectic at a later stage, because by giving arguments for both sides of a question it makes judgments about right and wrong less secure.[77] The model for government is to be taken especially from God himself, and from Christ who is both God and man, whose teachings will also be a principal source for instruction. Practice, which is the last part, is rather more hazardous in the case of a prince: for although it is of no great consequence if someone who is practising to become a good lutenist wears out a few lutes, it would indeed be a serious matter for the state to suffer while the prince learns how to administer it. By all means therefore let him get used to it from childhood onwards, by sitting in on consultations, by attending courts of law, by being present at the creation of magistrates, and by hearing the demands of kings; but this should all be after instruction in the principles involved, so that he may make a better appraisal. Let him not indeed decide anything without confirmation from the judgment of many others, until his age and experience have made his own judgment more reliable.

If Homer was right in saying that a prince cannot expect a full night's sleep, when so many thousands of people and such a great burden of business have been entrusted to him,[78] and if Virgil's similar picture of his Aeneas is aptly drawn,[79] then where does a prince find the leisure, I ask you, for wasting whole days on end,

[76] Plato, *Republic* 6.503 C–D and 8.547–8.
[77] Plato, *Republic* 7.539 A–B.
[78] Homer, *Iliad* 2.24–5.
[79] Virgil, *Aeneid* 1.305.

and indeed most of his life, in gambling, dancing, hunting, fooling about, and other even more trivial trivialities than these?

The state is being undermined by party rivalries and afflicted by wars, robbery is everywhere, the common people are reduced to starvation and the gallows by rampant extortion, the weak are oppressed by the injustice of those in high places, and corrupt magistrates do what they please instead of what the law says; and in the middle of this, is the prince playing dice as if he were on holiday?

The man at the helm cannot be a sleepyhead, so can the prince go snoring on in such perilous conditions? No sea ever has such severe storms as every kingdom constantly experiences. And the prince must therefore always be on his guard against going off course in some way, since he cannot go wrong without bringing disaster to thousands.

The size of his ship, the value of his cargo, or the number of his passengers are not the source of greater pride but of greater vigilance in a good ship's captain. So the more subjects a good king has, the more alert he must be, not the more arrogant.

If you reflect upon how great a kingdom you support, there will always be something to do; and if you get into the habit of taking pleasure in the well-being of the people, you will never be without a source of pleasure, so that there will then be no scope for idle boredom to distract the good prince with improper diversions. The prince must especially observe what has been laid down by the wisest men, that is, to choose that way of life which is the best, not the most attractive, because in the end familiarity generally makes what is best attractive too.

If an artist gets pleasure from a beautiful painting which he has done, and if a farmer, a market gardener, and a craftsmen enjoy their work, nothing should be more pleasurable for the prince than surveying a state which has been improved and made more prosperous by his own efforts.

While there is no denying that being a good prince is a burden, it is much more of a burden to be a bad one. Natural and reasonable things take far less trouble than simulations and deceptions.

If you are really a prince, it will be surprising if you do not feel a great glow of satisfaction when you think to yourself: 'I was wise to avoid that war, it was a good thing to stifle that uprising with the least possible bloodshed, and in approving that man as a magistrate I acted in the best interests of the state and of my reputation.' And this indeed is a pleasure worthy of the Christian prince; provide yourself with the raw material for it in your everyday acts of goodness and leave other vulgar little amusements to the worthless rabble.

Everybody praises Solomon because when he was in a position to ask for whatever he wanted and would have received at once whatever he asked, he did not ask for enormous wealth, or to rule the whole world, or for the destruction of his enemies, or for exceptional fame and glory, or for pleasure, but for wisdom; and not for just any wisdom, but for that which would enable him to govern creditably the kingdom entrusted to him.[80] Midas, on the other hand, is condemned by everybody because he valued nothing more than gold. And why should there be one judgment for history and another for real life? We want happiness for the prince, victory, praise, long life, and wealth; but if we really are devoted to the prince, why do we not rather desire for him the one thing that Solomon wanted? And in order to prevent his request from seeming foolish, God commended the wisdom of it, on this basis. Why should we regard the only thing which is relevant to something as being least relevant? And yet there are plenty of people who believe that the one thing which obstructs the function of government is having a wise prince. They say that the strength of his character is dissipated and he becomes too cautious. But they are talking about rashness, not courage; to lack fear because you lack judgment is not strength of mind but stupidity. Bravery in the prince must be sought from other sources; for by that standard young men are very brave, but people in a rage are even more so. A sense of fear is useful when it points out danger and teaches one to avoid it and when it restrains one from a shameful and corrupting way of life.

Someone who is on watch for everybody by himself has to be especially watchful, and someone who looks after the interests of everybody on his own has to be especially wise. What God is in the universe, what the sun is to the world, and what the eye is in the body, that must the prince be in the state.

[80] 1 Kings 3, 5–12.

Wise men of ancient times, whose way it was to use hieroglyphics and sketch the significance of things in a lifelike symbol, used to represent the image of a king in this way: they would draw an eye and add a sceptre, signifying integrity of life and a mind which is not to be diverted for any reason from what is right and which is equipped with sound judgment and the greatest vigilance.[81]

Others used to depict the royal sceptre in this way: at the top was a stork, the symbol of devotion to duty, and at the bottom a hippopotamus, a wild and dangerous animal.[82] This was to imply, as you can see, that, if ever wild emotions such as anger, desire for revenge, greed, or violence are raging in the prince then devotion to his country conquers and suppresses those feelings. Arrogance is encouraged by taking advantage of good fortune and by material success, but love for one's country should be stronger than these.

According to Plutarch, the Thebans in olden times used to have among their sacred images some seated figures without hands, and the chief of these also had no eyes. He tells us that the reason for their being seated is that magistrates and judges ought to have a calm temperament unruffled by any emotion. He suggests that they have no hands because they must be blameless and untouched by any corrupting bribe. Further, the fact that the chief one also has no eyes means that the king is so impervious to being bribed into dishonesty that he is not even affected by regard for any person's appearance and takes in information only with his ears.[83]

In the same vein, let the prince learn to take a philosophical interest in the very insignia with which he is adorned. What does the anointing of kings mean except great mildness of spirit? What does the crown on his head mean except a wisdom supreme among innumerable people? The interwoven chain put round his neck stands for the harmonious combination of all virtues; the jewels shining with multicoloured brilliance and beauty mean the perfection of virtue and that every kind of goodness must stand out in the prince; the glowing purple robes signify his intense affection towards his subjects; his official decorations indicate that he will

[81] Plutarch, *Moralia* 354 F and 371 E. See also *Adages* II.i.1.
[82] Plutarch, *Moralia* 962 E.
[83] Plutarch, *Moralia* 355 A. This example, together with the sceptre and the eye above, is also to be found in the adage 'Scarabeus aquilam quaerit' (III.vii.1).

either equal or surpass the achievements of his ancestors. The sword carried in front of him signifies that under his protection the country is to be safe, both from outside enemies and from crime within.[84]

The first obligation of the good prince is to have the best possible intentions; the next is to be on the look-out for ways of avoiding or removing evils, and, on the other hand, of achieving, increasing, and reinforcing what is good. It is perhaps enough for a private individual to be well intentioned, since he is guided by the law and the magistrates prescribe what is to be done. But in the prince it is not enough to be well meaning and have the best intentions, unless they are accompanied by wisdom, which demonstrates by what means he may achieve what he desires.

How little difference there is between a marble statue inscribed with the name of Croesus or Cyrus and superbly decked out with crown and sceptre and a prince who has no heart! The only difference is that the blank stare of the former does nobody any harm, while the latter's senselessness is very detrimental to the state.

Do not judge yourself by the qualities of your stature or your fortunate position but by those of the mind, and measure yourself not by the praises of other people but by your own actions.

Since you are the prince, see to it that you allow only such compliments as are worthy of a prince. If someone speaks highly of your appearance, reflect that that sort of praise is for a woman. If anyone admires your eloquence, remember that that is praise for sophists and orators. If anyone extols your strength and physical powers, bear in mind that that is how athletes are to be praised, not princes. If somebody praises your tall stature, think to yourself, 'He would be right to compliment me on this if something had to be reached down from a high place.' When someone has praise for your wealth, be sure to think that that is the way for businessmen to be praised. Consider that you have still heard nothing suitable for a prince so long as you are hearing fanfares of this sort. What praise, then, is proper for princes? Well, certainly if he has eyes at the back as well as at the front and can look forwards and backwards, as Homer says; that is, if he knows the most that is possible, looking back on

---

[84] These symbolic meanings for royal regalia were regularly invoked in descriptions of royal coronations down to the twentieth century. This whole section is heavily influenced by Plutarch's *Moralia*.

what has happened and forward to the future, and then if he uses whatever he knows for his country's good and not his own.[85] And yet there is no other way of increasing his wisdom for himself than by using it for his country.

Suppose that someone praises a physician along these lines: 'He is good-looking and well-built, he has good family connections, he is well off, he is good with the dice, he is an accomplished dancer, he sings beautifully and he is a skilful ball-player'; would you not immediately think to yourself, 'What has this to do with being a physician?' And when you hear the same things from foolish eulogisers, then reflect all the more, 'What has this to do with being a prince?'

There are three principal requirements in a medical man: first, that he be skilled in the curative arts and familiar with the resources of the body, the powers of diseases, and the treatment to use for each illness; second, that he should be sincere and not have his eye on anything except the health of the patient, for many are led on by ambition or money to the point of administering poison instead of medicine; third, that he should pay close attention and take the necessary pains. But these things are of much greater importance for the prince.

Finally, what does Aristotle, a pagan, demand in the prince in his *Politics*?[86] The beauty of Nereus? The strength of Milo? The stature of Maximinus? The wealth of Tantalus? No, none of these. What then? He expects the highest and most complete integrity, even though he is content with a moderate standard in private individuals.

If you can be a prince and a good man at the same time, you will be performing a magnificent service; but if not, give up the position of prince rather than become a bad man for the sake of it. It is quite possible to find a good man who would not make a good prince, yet one cannot be a good prince without at the same time being a good man. However the standards of some princes have now reached the point where these two roles of good man and prince seem to be very much in conflict with each other, and it is regarded as patently foolish and ridiculous to speak of a good man and a prince in the same breath.

[85] Homer, *Iliad* 1.343 and 3.109.
[86] Aristotle, *Politics* 3.11.12 and 1.5.7.

You will not be able to be a king unless reason is king over you; that is, unless you follow good sense and balanced judgment rather than personal desires in all things. Nor can you rule over others unless you yourself have previously obeyed what is right.

Let that more than tyrannical slogan, 'I desire this, I command this, let my will be the reason,' be far removed from the mind of the prince.[87] And much more so the one which has already met with the general condemnation of mankind, 'Let them hate me so long as they fear me.'[88] It is the mark of a tyrant, and indeed of a woman, to follow an emotional impulse, and fear is a very bad protector for any length of time.

Let it be the prince's constant principle to harm nobody, to be of help to everybody, especially his own people, and either to tolerate such faults as there are or to put them right according to his assessment of what is expedient for the common good. Anyone who does not have this attitude towards the state is a tyrant, not a prince.

If anyone were to call you not a prince but a tyrant and a robber, would you not be enraged and instigate terrible punishment for him? And rightly so: for it is a terrible insult, and one which should not be put up with in any circumstances. But I would like you to consider this point: how much more of an insult directed against himself is it for someone to choose to be the kind of man he is accused of being? For it is a more serious matter to be a thief than to be called one, and it is more brutal to violate a young girl than to be accused of the violation.

In order to be well spoken of, the most reliable course to follow is to show yourself to be the sort of person that you want men to call you. It is not genuine praise that is extracted by intimidation or offered by flatterers, and it is detrimental to the prince's reputation if its protection depends upon silence induced by threats. Although your own age may keep very quiet at the moment, posterity will surely speak. Was there ever any tyrant so terrifying that he could seal the lips of absolutely everybody?

The Christian prince must take especial care on a point which Seneca has wisely discussed. Among those who are called kings, some can be found who, even in comparison with Phalaris, Dionys-

---

[87] Juvenal, *Satires* 6.223.
[88] See Erasmus's *Adages* ii.ix.62.

ius, and Polycrates (whose very names have become objects of disgust in every century), do not deserve to be called so much as tyrants. For it is not a question of which road you are on, but in which direction you are going: he who looks to the common good is a king; he who looks to his own good is a tyrant. And yet what name shall we then assign to those who feather their own nests at their country's expense, and who are in fact robbers although in name (but falsely so) princes?[89]

In his laws, Plato forbids anyone to say that God is the source of any evil, because he is by nature good and beneficent.[90] But the prince is a kind of representation of God, if he is a true prince. How far, then, do rulers fall short of this ideal if they act in such a way that whatever evils arise in the state arise from their own defects?

Pay no attention if some flatterer should object at this point that this amounts to reducing the prince to the ranks. Not at all: it is the one who wants to allow the prince to act disreputably who is reducing him to the ranks. For what else is reducing the prince to the ranks apart from turning him into the same sort of person as the man in the street, so that he is at the mercy of anger, desire, ambition, greed, and foolishness? Would it really be shameful and intolerable if what is not allowed to God is not allowed to the prince? God does not ask to be allowed to please himself so that he may ignore what good principles dictate: if he did this he would not then be God. Consequently, someone who wants to allow this to the prince when it conflicts with the nature and principles of being a prince is ultimately depriving him of princely status and making him just one of the common crowd. The prince should not be ashamed to obey what is good and right, for God himself obeys it; nor should he think himself any less a prince if he makes every effort to approach the image of the highest prince of all.

To produce a good prince, these and similar seeds should be sown from the start by parents, nurses, and tutor in the boy's young mind; and let him learn them voluntarily and not under compulsion. For this is the way to bring up a prince who is destined to rule over

[89] Seneca, *De clementia* 1.12.1.
[90] Plato, *Republic* 2.380 B–C.

free and willing subjects. Let him learn to love goodness, to shun depravity, and to keep away from corrupt influences out of decency and not out of fear. And although some hope of developing a good prince lies in changed behaviour and the control of feelings, nevertheless the chief hope is in correct beliefs. For sometimes even a bad conscience checks bad behaviour, and either maturity or reproach corrects debased inclinations. But when there is the conviction that something utterly dishonourable has its merits and that something more than tyrannical is an outstanding quality in the prince (that is, when the sources from which all life's actions flow are contaminated), then the remedy is very difficult. Consequently the educator must be primarily and especially concerned, as has been said, on this point: to eradicate from his pupil's mind whatever shameful and vulgar ideas may somehow have taken root, and to implant those that are healthy and worthy of the Christian prince.[91]

2 *The prince must avoid flatterers*

The prince must avoid flatterers; but this cannot be brought about unless flatterers are kept at bay by every means, for the well-being of great princes is extremely vulnerable to this particular plague. Youthful innocence in itself is particularly exposed to this evil, partly because of the natural inclination to enjoy compliments more than the truth, and partly because of inexperience: the less suspicious the prince is of trickery, the less he knows about taking precautions.[92]

And in case anyone thinks that this can be ignored as a trivial misfortune, he should realise that the most flourishing empires of the greatest kings have been overthrown by the flatterer's tongue. Nowhere do we read of a state oppressed by implacable tyranny without a flatterer playing a leading part in the tragedy.

---

[91] The programme which Erasmus has here outlined is deliberately presented so that it may be appropriately adopted for the education of any boy whose future involves governing the lives of others, i.e. any boy from an elite family.

[92] This section concerns advisers to princes—the sort of post to which Erasmus had himself recently been appointed by Charles when he wrote *The Education of a Christian Prince*. In this chapter Erasmus borrows extensively from Plutarch's essay on 'How to distinguish a friend from a flatterer', which he had translated for and dedicated to the English king Henry VIII, and which was reprinted with the first edition of the *Education of a Christian Prince*.

Unless I am mistaken, this is what Diogenes had in mind when he replied to the question 'What is the most dangerous animal of all?' 'If you mean wild animals', he said, 'the tyrant; if you mean tame ones, a flatterer.'[93] This pest has a certain attractive poison, but it acts so quickly that once the princes who rule the world are deranged by it they have allowed themselves to become the play-things of the most vile flatterers and to be taken for a ride by them; these repulsively depraved little men, and sometimes even slaves, were masters of the masters of the world.

In the first place, therefore, it will be necessary to see that nurses are employed who are either completely immune to this disease or at any rate the least susceptible to it. For their very sex tends to make them especially vulnerable to this evil; then again, most nurses take on the emotional tendencies of mothers, the majority of whom frequently spoil the characters of their children by over-indulgence. Indeed, this whole group should be kept away from the future prince as far as possible, since they have inherited more or less in their very nature the two great faults of foolishness and flattery.[94]

The next concern will be to provide him with well-bred companions (though they will also need some grooming to this end from his tutor) to become his friends but not his flatterers and to create an atmosphere of civilised talk without ever using pretence or lies to gain favour. As to the choice of the tutor, I have already spoken about that.

The question of the prince's attendants is not an insignificant one either, for they often pander to a boy's predilections, either through stupidity or in the hope that some sort of recompense will come their way. It will therefore be necessary to fill these positions as far as possible with men who are prudent and honest, and beyond that to deter them by means of warnings and threats from being too permissive, and even further to use rewards to induce them to perform their function conscientiously. This cause will indeed be greatly advanced if anyone who has been caught giving encouragement and ignoble subservience in such a way as to spur the prince's

---

[93] Plutarch, *Moralia* 61 C (it was Bias, in fact, not Diogenes who made the observation). 'Unless I am mistaken' implies that Erasmus here as elsewhere is quoting from memory.

[94] This is virtually all Erasmus has to say about women's role in raising the future prince.

mind towards things that are beneath the dignity of a prince is punished in public as an example to others (even by death if the nature of his offence requires it). Since we have the death penalty (and that beyond all the laws of the ancients) for a thief who steals a bit of money that he has come across, it ought not to seem cruel to anyone if the ultimate penalty is invoked for someone who has tried to corrupt the best and most precious thing that the country possesses. But the novelty of the idea may prevent its acceptance, although the Roman emperor Alexander ordered a seller of empty promises called Thurinus to be bound to a stake and smoked to death by green logs set alight at his feet. In that case, it might be possible to construct an example artificially by finding a man who has already been convicted of some other capital offence and having it advertised that he was executed for contaminating the mind of the future prince with the plague of flattery.

If in fixing the penalty one is to take account of the harm done, then a plague of a flatterer does more damage to the state by corrupting and contaminating those first years of the prince with the ideas of a tyrant than does someone who steals from the public treasury. Anyone who has debased the prince's coinage is visited with ingeniously devised punishments, whereas there seems almost to be a reward for those who debase the prince's mind.

If only that dictum of Carneades were less true at least among us Christians: he said that royal sons could not learn anything properly except horse-riding because in all other things everybody humoured and flattered them, but since a mere horse doesn't know whether he is being ridden by a nobleman or a commoner, by a rich man or a poor man, by a prince or a private individual, he throws off his back anyone who rides him incompetently.[95] But it is a fact, as we too often see, that not only do nurses, companions, and attendants flatter a prince's children, but even the very tutor who has been trusted to form the boy's character conducts his business with a view not to passing out a better prince but to walking out a richer man himself. Quite often even those who preach on religious matters speak ingratiatingly, fishing for the favour of the prince and his court, or if they have some criticism to make, they mouth it in such a way that it becomes the greatest flattery. I do not say this because

---

[95] Plutarch, *Moralia* 58 F. See also Erasmus, *Apophthegms*.

I think that the use of inflammatory language to rant against the lives of princes should be encouraged, but because I would like preachers to put forward a positive example of a good prince without abuse and not to approve in the Christian prince by obsequious connivance what the pagans have condemned in pagan princes. Officers of state do not give frank advice and counsellors do not consult with him with enough openness of heart. For since the nobility have rival interests among themselves, they all vie with one another in courting the prince's approval, either to put down an opponent or to avoid providing an enemy with a rod for their own backs. The priests are flatterers and the physicians are yes-men. It is now the custom everywhere to listen to undiluted praise from orators sent from abroad. There used to be one sheet-anchor remaining, but even that is now unreliable: I mean of course those whom the common people call 'royal confessors'. If they were sincere and prudent, surely they would be able to give the prince friendly and sincere advice in that uttermost privacy which they enjoy. And yet it very often happens that while each one is looking out for his own interests the means of serving the common good are neglected. Less harm indeed is done by poets and orators, who are all by now well versed in the practice of taking the measure for a prince's praise not from his deserts but from their own inspiration. Far more damaging are people like magicians and soothsayers who promise kings long life, victory, triumphs, pleasures, and kingdoms and then again threaten others with sudden death, disaster, affliction, and exile, trading upon hope and fear, the two chief tyrants of human life, in the process. Astrologers, who foretell the future from the stars, belong to the same class, but this is not the place to discuss whether theirs is a genuine science. Certainly, however, the hold they now have over the ordinary man presents no small problem to humanity.[96]

But the most pernicious flatterers of all are those who operate with apparent frankness but in some remarkable way contrive to urge you on while seeming to restrain you and to praise you while seeming to criticise. Plutarch has portrayed them marvellously in a

---

[96] See also Erasmus, *Panegyric*. More takes a similarly dim view of astrologers in the second book of *Utopia*. This section of Erasmus's treatise approaches closest to the social satire of More's little work.

short essay entitled 'How to distinguish a friend from a flatterer.'[97]

Now there are two times of life which are especially vulnerable to flattery: childhood because of inexperience and old age because of mental impairment. Folly, however, appears at any age and always brings self-love along with it. And Plato was right to warn us that the most dangerous kind of flattery is when someone is his own flatterer and as a result readily lays himself open to other people doing the same thing as he himself did of his own accord.

There is a certain implicit flattery in portraits, statues, and inscriptions.[98] Thus Apelles flattered Alexander the Great by painting him brandishing a thunderbolt; and Octavius enjoyed being painted in the likeness of Apollo. The same thing goes for those huge 'colossus' statues, greater than life-size, which they used to erect to emperors in the past. A point that may seem trivial to some people, but is nevertheless of considerable importance here, is that artists should represent the prince in the dress and manner that is most worthy of a wise and distinguished prince. And it is preferable to depict him engaged in some aspect of state business rather than at leisure: for example, Alexander holding a hand over one ear while he attends to a trial, or Darius holding a pomegranate, or Scipio restoring to a young man his betrothed wife untouched and rejecting the gold which was offered to him. It is right that the halls of princes should be decorated with fine pictures of this sort, and not with those that encourage debauchery, arrogance, or tyranny.

Now as regards honorary titles, I would not myself deny to the prince his tribute of respect, but I would prefer them to be of such a kind that they remind the prince in some way of his office: that is, I would prefer him to be called Most Honourable, Most Blameless, Most Wise, Most Merciful, Most Beneficent, Most Prudent, Most Watchful, Most Temperate, Most Patriotic; rather than the Famous, the Invincible, the Triumphant, the Ever-August, not to mention the 'Highnesses', 'Sacred Majesties', 'Divinities', and even more flattering titles than these. I approve of the present custom honouring the Roman pontiff with the title 'his Holiness' because by hearing it continually he is reminded in what way he ought to

---

[97] Published with the first edition of *The Education of a Christian Prince*.

[98] Another veiled criticism of the artistic patronage of Renaissance princes.

excel and what is his finest quality: not having great wealth or a far-flung empire, but being pre-eminent in holiness.[99]

But if it is inevitable that the prince should hear this sort of title sometimes, even against his will, nevertheless he ought not to hide his feelings about what would please him better. Alexander Severus is said to have regarded all flatterers with such hatred that if anybody saluted him too obsequiously or bowed his head too humbly, he would at once noisily denounce the man and send him packing; and if a man's rank or office saved him from loud denunciation, he was rebuked by a grim countenance.

The boy must therefore be instructed in advance to turn those titles which he is forced to hear to his own advantage. When he hears 'Father of His Country', let him reflect that no title given to princes more precisely squares with being a good prince than does 'Father of His Country'; consequently he must act in such a way that he is seen to be worthy of that title. If he thinks in this way, it will have been a reminder; if not, flattery.

When he is called 'Invincible', let him think how absurd it is to call invincible a man who is conquered by anger, a slave to lust every single day, and the prisoner of ambition, which leads and drives him where it likes. He should think a man truly invincible only when he does not give in to any emotion and cannot be deflected from what is right by any circumstance.

When he is designated 'Serene', let it come to mind that it is the prince's duty to keep everything peaceful and harmonious. But if anyone disrupts and confuses the order of things by revolts and the upheavals of war, whether out of ambition or anger, the title of 'the Serene' is no ornament for him but flings his crime in his face.

When he is called 'the Famous', let him reflect that no accolade is valid except that which arises from integrity and good actions. For if anyone is depraved by desire, corrupted by greed, or defiled by ambition, then the title 'the Famous' is nothing but a warning

---

[99] With this last comment Erasmus carefully avoids direct criticism of the supreme pontiff, although many of the other titles he cites were also applied to popes like Leo X who exercised secular as well as sacred dominion in Europe. Erasmus dedicated his *Novum instrumentum* (his controversial revised text of the New Testament, published in 1516) to Leo X, who he hoped would provide him with ecclesiastical protection and patronage.

if he is going astray inadvertently, or a condemnation if he knows he is doing wrong.

When he hears the names of his territories, let him not immediately swell with pride at being the master of such great affairs, but let him reflect what a multitude they are to whom he must be a good prince.[100]

If anyone offers him 'your Highness', 'your Majesty', 'the Divine', he will remember that these are valid only for someone who governs his realm according to the example of God with a kind of heavenly magnanimity.

When he listens to solemn eulogies, let him not immediately believe or approve of such praise of himself, but if he is not yet such a person as they make him out to be, let him regard it as an admonition and energetically pursue the goal of some day living up to that praise. If he already is such a person, he must strive to improve upon himself.

Indeed even the laws themselves will have to be held under suspicion, for even they sometimes collude with the prince; and no wonder, because they have been either collated or instituted by those who were under the thumb of kings or emperors. When they say that the prince is above the law, when they submit themselves to him, and when they accord him jurisdiction over all things, he must beware that he does not immediately get the idea that he is allowed to do whatever he pleases. To a good prince you can safely allow everything, to an average one not everything, to a bad one nothing.

Demetrius Phalereus shrewdly recommends the prince to read books, because very often he may learn from these what his friends have not dared to bring to his attention.[101] But in this matter he must be equipped in advance with an antidote, as it were, along these lines: 'This writer whom you are reading is a pagan and you are a Christian reader; although he has many excellent things to say, he nevertheless does not depict the ideal of a Christian prince quite accurately, and you must take care not to think that whatever you come across at any point is to be imitated straight away, but instead test everything against the standard of Christ.'

---

[100] A remark directed specifically at Charles, whose territories stretched right across Europe.

[101] Plutarch, *Moralia* 189 D. See also Erasmus, *Apophthegms*.

But first, indeed, comes the selection of authors, for it matters a great deal what books a boy reads and absorbs first. Bad conversation defiles the mind, and bad reading does so no less. For those silent letters are transformed into conduct and feelings, especially if they have taken hold of the mind which is prone to some defect; for example, it will take very little to incite a naturally wild and violent boy to tyranny if, without being equipped with an antidote, he reads about Achilles or Alexander the Great or Xerxes or Julius Caesar.

But today we see a great many people enjoying the stories of Arthur and Lancelot and other legends of that sort, which are not only tyrannical but also utterly illiterate, foolish, and on the level of old wives' tales, so that it would be more advisable to put one's reading time into the comedies or the myths of the poets rather than into that sort of drivel.[102]

But if any tutor wants my advice, as soon as the boy has a grasp of language he should present the proverbs of Solomon, Ecclesiasticus, and the Book of Wisdom, not so that the lad is tormented by the notorious four senses at the hands of a meretricious interpreter, but so that he may be shown briefly and conveniently whatever is relevant to the office of a good prince.[103] In the first place a liking for the writer and his work must be inculcated. 'You are destined for kingship', one can say. 'This author teaches the art of being a king. You are the son of a king and a future king yourself; you will hear what the wisest king of all teaches his own son whom he is preparing for succession to the throne.' Next the Gospels; and here it is very important in what way you kindle a love of the author and the work in the boy's mind. For a good deal will depend upon the interpreter's ingenuity and fluency in communicating concisely, clearly, convincingly, and even excitingly not everything, but those things which are particularly relevant to the prince's role and which serve to rid his mind of the dangerous attitudes of commonplace

---

[102] Erasmus's negative opinion of romances was shared by many other humanist educators. Because of his upbringing at the Burgundian Court, Prince Charles was probably more familiar with the romances of Arthur and Lancelot than with the Greek and Latin classics which humanist tutors were reading with their pupils in Italy and elsewhere.

[103] In other words, the boy prince should read the Scriptures for their sense, and the wisdom they contain, not as a theologian, analysing the text for theological argument.

princes. Thirdly, the *Apophthegms* of Plutarch and then his *Moralia*; for you can find nothing sounder than these, and I would prefer his *Lives* to be prescribed rather than those of anyone else. The next place after Plutarch I would readily assign to Seneca, for his writings excite and inspire the reader in a wonderful way to cultivate integrity and lift his spirit high above worldly concerns, especially in their repeated denunciation of tyranny. A good many extracts very worthy of attention can properly be taken from the *Politics* of Aristotle and the *Offices* of Cicero but, in my opinion, Plato has the purer message on this subject, and Cicero followed him to some extent in his book on *The Laws* (for the latter's *Republic* is lost). Now I would not deny, to be sure, that very considerable wisdom can be gathered from reading the historians, but you will also take in the most destructive ideas from these same writers unless you are forearmed and read selectively. See that you are not misled by the names of writers and leaders celebrated by the agreed judgment of the ages. Both Herodotus and Xenophon were pagans and very often depict the worst image of a prince, even if in doing so they were writing history, whether telling an enjoyable story or painting a picture of an outstanding leader. Much of what Sallust and Livy write is indeed admirable, and, I would add, all of it is scholarly, but they do not approve of everything that they recount and they approve of some things which should by no means be approved of by a Christian prince. When you hear of Achilles, Xerxes, Cyrus, Darius, or Julius, do not be at all overwhelmed by the enormous prestige of their names; you are hearing about great raging bandits, for that is what Seneca calls them several times.[104]

Yet if you come across anything in these men's actions which is worthy of the good prince, you will take care to rescue it like a jewel from a dung-heap. For no tyrant was ever so completely blameworthy that he was not involved in some things, among everything else, which can at least be fitted into a demonstration of virtue, even though they were not the products of virtue. There are many things

---

[104] This time Erasmus does insist that the prince's instruction should begin with the Old and New Testaments. The list of pagan works with which he continues are those from which he cites most frequently in the course of this treatise. It is particularly striking that Plutarch's works head the list, followed by Seneca. Both are lynch-pins of Erasmus's moral and political theory. Aristotle's *Politics* comes some way behind, and are paired with another of Erasmus's (and other humanists') favourites, Cicero's *Offices*.

in the letters of Phalaris which seem to be quite worthy of any good king, and the way in which he had Perillus, who was the architect of cruelty, hoist with his own petard is a good enough lesson in kingship.[105] Alexander acted wildly in many ways, but he was right not to touch the women he had captured from Darius and he was right to order a woman to be taken back home when he found out that she was married. These passages, then, will have to be selected from much else; examples taken from the pagans and from despicable men can still be intensely inspiring. If a tyrant and a non-Christian was able to show such restraint, and if a youthful conqueror showed this honourable attitude toward the enemy's women, what ought my attitude to be as a Christian prince toward mine? If a mere girl had so much spirit, what is to be expected from a man? If something was condemned in a pagan prince by the pagans, how keenly must I strive to avoid it since I profess the religion of Christ!

Beyond this, I think I have pointed out frequently how to accumulate examples by expansion in my book *De copia*.[106] Even examples of vice, however, can be turned to the good: the energy and high-mindedness of Julius Caesar, which he prostituted to his ambition, you could well devote to the interests of your country, and the clemency which he simulated for the sake of winning and maintaining the position of tyrant you should use in all sincerity to winning over your subjects' affection to yourself.

Indeed the examples of the worst princes are sometimes more of an incentive to virtue than are those of the best or average rulers. For anyone would be dissuaded from greed by the story of Vespasian's tax on urine and by his statement (no less disgusting than the facts) 'money smells good wherever it comes from'; and the same goes for that detestable phrase of Nero with which he used to instruct his officers: 'You·know what I want, and see that nobody else keeps any.' In these ways you will be able to turn anything encountered in the historians into an example of proper conduct.

---

[105] The letters of Phalaris is another work much vaunted by humanist moralists.

[106] Erasmus's *De copia* (published 1512) was probably his most famous and most read secular work. Its stated aim is to train students in Latin eloquence, providing them with extensive literary material on a wide range of moral topics. It is significant that Erasmus refers to it here as if the activity of making students fluent in elegant Latin is also one of moral and political preparation for a life of responsibility.

For your commanders, be sure that you choose the best from the great multitude of examples, such as Aristides, Epaminondas, Octavius, Trajan, Antoninus Pius, Alexander Mammeas. Nevertheless, you would not want to emulate them in their entirety but to pick out for yourself the best in the best of them; conversely, there are features that you would avoid even in David and Solomon, two kings who were praised by God.

On the other hand, what greater madness could there be than for a man who has received the Christian sacraments to model himself on Alexander, Julius Caesar, or Xerxes, whose lives even the pagan writers criticised (or those of them who had some degree of judgment)? Just as it would be an utter disgrace to be surpassed by them in any of their good actions, so for a Christian prince to want to copy them completely would be sheer insanity.

The prince must be forewarned not to think that he should imitate straight away even what he reads in the Scriptures. He should learn that the battles and carnage of the Hebrews and their savage cruelty to their enemies are to be interpreted allegorically; otherwise they make pernicious reading. There is a vast difference between what was permitted to that people in accordance with the standards of the time and what is laid down for the blessed company of Christians.[107]

Whenever the prince takes a book in his hands, let him do it not for the purpose of enjoyment but in order that he may get up from his reading a better man.[108] Anyone who strives energetically to improve himself soon finds out how to do so. A considerable part of goodness is the wish to achieve it: for example, someone who recognises in himself the disease of ambition or truculence or lust, who hates what he sees, and who opens a book looking for a remedy for his malady readily discovers how the affliction may be either banished or mitigated.

Nobody speaks the truth more honestly or more advantageously or more candidly than do books; but the prince must nevertheless accustom his friends to the knowledge that they find favour by giving frank advice. It is indeed the job of those who keep the prince

---

[107] Erasmus here cautions that the lessons of the Old Testament are not to be taken as literally as those of the New.

[108] A classic formulation of the humanist assumption that learning necessarily improves the one who learns.

company to advise him opportunely, advantageously, and amicably, but it will nevertheless be well to forgive those whose advice is presented clumsily in order that no precedent may deter those who would advise him properly from doing their duty.

In a severe storm, even the most skilful sailor accepts advice from someone else; but a kingdom is never without its storm. Who could adequately commend the social judgment which Philip of Macedon displayed when he granted freedom to the man who secretly advised him that he looked indecent when he was sitting with his cloak drawn up to the knee?[109] What he did in a trivial matter the prince must do much more in matters which are hazardous for the country, such as undertaking foreign visits, revising the laws, entering into treaties, and declaring war.

3 The arts of peace

Although ancient writers divided the whole theory of statecraft into two sets of skills, those of peace and of war, our first and foremost concern must be for training the prince in the skills relevant to wise administration in time of peace, because with them he must strive to his utmost for this end: that the devices of war may never be needed.[110]

On this point indeed, it seems necessary for the prince to learn above all to get to know his kingdom, and this achievement will be most effectively brought about by three things: the study of geography, the study of history, and frequent tours of towns and territories. So let him take particular care to become familiar with the location of territories and cities, their history, natural character, institutions, customs, laws, records, and rights. No one can cure the body unless he understands it; nobody farms a field properly which he does not know. It is true that the tyrant also studies these things very closely, but it is in the motive rather than the action that the good prince differs: a doctor investigates the workings of the body in order that he may the more readily come to its aid; a poisoner also studies them, but so as to be more certain to kill.[111]

[109] Plutarch, *Moralia* 178 C–D. See also Erasmus, *Apophthegms*.
[110] See also More's *Utopia*, book I. Erasmus believed passionately that only in times of peace could humane learning and civilised values flourish.
[111] The advice in this paragraph is particularly directed at the Habsburgs.

The next lesson is to love the country he rules and to have the same attitude towards it that a good farmer has towards the land he has inherited or that a good man has towards his family, and to be especially concerned that he will hand over to whoever comes next an improvement on what he himself received. If there are children, let the prince as father be guided by his duty towards them; if there are not, let his duty to his country be his guide, and let his patriotism, like a torch, continually inspire him to keep alive his affection for his subjects. Let him think of his kingdom as being like some great body of which he himself is a vital part, and that people who have committed all their fortunes and their security to the good faith of one individual deserve benevolent consideration. Let him frequently call to mind the example of those who have held the well-being of their citizens more precious than their own lives and lastly let him consider that it is impossible for a prince to harm the state without harming himself.

Next, he will make every kind of effort to gain affection from the people in his turn, but in such a way that his authority among them is in no way diminished. There are indeed those who are foolish enough to try to win good will for themselves with incantations and magic rings, when no spell is more effective than virtue itself and nothing more desirable, and, since it is a true good and has no end, so it wins a man true and endless good will. A second 'potion' is for a man to show love to others if he wants to be loved in return, so that he binds his citizens to him in the same way that God draws all the world together to himself, by deserving well of them.

Those who court the affections of the common people with handouts, feasts, and shameful indulgence are also misguided, since these things achieve a certain popularity rather than good will, and indeed a popularity that is insincere and short-lived. Meanwhile the vicious greed of the populace is fostered, and they come to think, after it has grown to enormous proportions (which is what happens), that nothing is enough, and they become unruly if their selfish demands are not met at every point. That is to make your people corrupt, not to make them loyal. And by this means the same things tend to happen to the prince among his people as happens to foolish husbands who wheedle from their wives, with flattery, presents, and subservience the love which they ought to win by their good qualities and upright behaviour. For what happens eventually is that they are not loved and that they have fussy and ungovernable wives instead of thrifty and orderly ones; instead of obedient wives, complaining nuisances. Or, as it usually turns out with those women who try with drugs to force their husbands to love them, they get maniacs instead of rational men.

First let the wife learn the ways and qualities by which to tell that a husband is worth loving, then let him be seen to be the sort of person who can rightly be loved. In the same way, let the people get a taste for the best and let the prince show that he is of the best. They love long whose love was well judged to begin with.

So let the prince who wants to be loved by his people first of all show himself to be someone who deserves to be loved; next it will be a considerable advantage to pursue a policy by which he may insinuate himself more securely into the hearts of all. Let the prince do this first, so that the best people regard him most favourably, and so that he is approved of by those whom everybody approves; let him have these people as his closest associates, admit them into his councils, decorate them with honours, allow them to have the greatest influence with him. In this way it will soon come about that everyone will have the highest possible opinion of the prince, who is the source of all the good will. I have known princes who were not particularly bad in themselves but who encountered public hostility for the simple reason that they allowed too much licence to people held in low esteem by the general populace, and the latter judged the character of the princes from these men's behaviour.

For my part, I prefer a prince to be born and brought up among the people he is to rule, for mutual regard develops and consolidates best whenever good will springs from a natural source.[112] The common people recoil from and hate the unknown even when it is good; and, conversely, evils that are familiar are sometimes held dear. This recommendation will bring two advantages: for not only will the prince be better disposed towards his people and altogether regard them more as his own, but also the people will support him more sincerely and more readily acknowledge him as their prince. And for this reason I am opposed to the currently accepted alliance of princes with foreign countries, and especially when they are far

[112] See the extravagant protestations of love and loyalty towards Philip expressed by Erasmus in his *Panegyric*.

away.[113] Ties of race and motherland and a certain instinct, as it were, common to both sides have great power to foster good will. A good part of this necessarily disappears when mixed marriages contaminate this intrinsic, inborn fellow-feeling. But where nature has laid the foundations of a mutual affection, it will be advantageous to increase and strengthen it repeatedly in other ways. Where it is absent, however, a more intense effort must be made to ensure that good will may be reinforced by acts of service to each other and by conduct worthy of approval. But as in marriage, when the wife initially submits to her husband and the man to some extent gives way to and humours his wife until the bonds of affection are gradually strengthened as they get to know one another, so the same thing should happen when a prince is adopted from another country. Mithridates had learned the languages of all the countries he ruled, which are said to have amounted to twenty-two.[114] In his dealings with other peoples, however barbarous, Alexander the Great began by taking over their customs and ways of life and endeared himself to them in this way. Alcibiades had the same praiseworthy characteristic.

Nothing alienates the people's affection from a prince as much as when he enjoys going abroad, because they seem to be being neglected by the one whom they would wish to be especially concerned for them. Then they regard the tax revenue that is exacted from them as being lost to themselves, because it is then spent elsewhere; and they do not think of it as being given to the prince but as being thrown away as plunder for foreigners. For this reason nothing is more harmful and damaging for the country or more dangerous for a prince than tours far afield, especially prolonged ones. For it was this, in everyone's view, that deprived us of Philip[115] and afflicted his kingdom just as much as the already protracted war with the Gelderlanders.[116]

---

[113] Power politics in Europe throughout the sixteenth century depended on fragile alliances between the rulers of the major territories—in particular the Habsburgs, Tudors, and Valois.

[114] Charles spoke few of the vernacular languages of the territories over which he ruled. He adopted Spanish as the official vernacular of his court.

[115] Philip the Fair, Prince Charles's father, who had died prematurely in 1506. Erasmus's *Panegyric* was written for Philip's return from a two-year absence from the Low Countries, visiting France, Spain and Germany; Erasmus delivered it in person before him in January 1504.

[116] Karl van Egmond, duke of Gelderland, who had been at war with the Habsburgs on and off since 1492. See Tracy, *Politics*, 12–13.

Just as the king bee is in the centre surrounded by the ranks and does not fly out anywhere, and as the heart is embedded in the body, so should the prince always be actively involved with his people.

According to Aristotle's *Politics*, there are two things which especially undermine government—hatred and contempt: good will is the opposite of hatred; authority, of contempt.[117] It will therefore be the prince's duty to keep a careful look-out for ways of cultivating the former and avoiding the latter. Hatred is incited by brutality, violence, insults, sullenness, obstinacy, and greed; and it is easier to provoke it than to mollify it once aroused. So the good prince must take every precaution against falling out of favour with his subjects for any reason. Believe me, the man who is deprived of the people's good will is stripped of much protection. On the other hand, good will is fostered, generally speaking, by those qualities most lacking in the tyrant: mercy, friendliness, fairness, courtesy, compassion. Benevolence encourages people to public service, especially if they have discerned that there is a royal reward for those who deserve well of the state. Mercy invites those who have a bad conscience to turn over a new leaf, while to those who may be trying to atone for the faults of their previous life by reformed behaviour it offers hope of forgiveness, and it provides at the same time an attractive image of human nature even to those of the most impeccable conduct. Everywhere courtesy either engenders affection or at least mollifies hatred, and to the people it is by far the most acceptable quality in a great prince.

Contempt is especially engendered by pursuit of pleasure, self-indulgence, drunkenness, feastings, gaming, the company of fools and parasites, and also by stupidity and negligence. And respect is achieved by opposite qualities: good judgment, honesty, restraint, sobriety, and alertness. Therefore let a prince who really wants to grow in authority with his people take these things to heart.

But some have the absurd belief that the way to be valued by their subjects is to display themselves with the greatest possible clamour, pomp, and extravagance; for who has a high regard for a prince laden with gold and jewels when everyone knows that as much as he wants is his? And in any case, what else is he displaying but the misfortune of his own citizens who are supplying his

---

[117] Aristotle, *Politics* 5.8.8.

extravagance at their own expense? Lastly, what is he teaching his people in this way except the origins of all evil-doing?

Let the good prince be brought up and live in such a way that the rest of the people, both noblemen and commoners, can take his life as a model of economy and moderation.

At home, let him conduct himself in such a way that nobody's interruption catches him off duty; outside, let nobody see the prince unless he is carrying out some public service the whole time.

The nature of the prince is recognised more surely from what he says than from what he wears: anything caught from the prince's lips is spread abroad. He must continually take the greatest care that what he says savours of integrity and gives evidence of thinking that is worthy of a good prince.

Nor should Aristotle's advice on this point be overlooked, that a prince who wants to escape his people's hatred and to develop their good will will delegate to others the tasks which the people resent and will carry out personally those that are well received.[118] By this means a good deal of the resentment will be diverted towards those who are administering that business, especially if the populace resented them on other grounds, and moreover, unreserved gratitude will accrue to the prince alone in his beneficent actions.

I would add this too, that the gratitude for a favour given is doubled by giving it quickly, with enthusiasm and without being asked, and with friendly words of commendation; and that when anything has to be refused, it should be done calmly and gently. If some punishment is to be given, the penalty prescribed by the law should be somewhat reduced and the sentence carried out in such a way that the prince gives the impression of having been driven to it against his will.

And it is not enough for the prince to show the state that his own personal character is sound and blameless: he must strive just as much to have, as far as possible, his whole entourage (nobles, friends, advisers, magistrates) like himself. They are the prince's agents, and hatred provoked by their faults rebounds against the prince himself. But it will be said that this is very difficult. It will prove quite simple, if he is careful to select the best people for his court, and if he has made sure that they understand that the prince

---

[118] Aristotle, *Politics* 5.9.16.

is most pleased by those things that are most in the interest of the people. Otherwise, it often happens that if the prince does not know about their actions, or even connives at them, the most wicked can impose a tyranny on the people under cover of the prince, and while they seem to be carrying out his business, they can do the greatest disservice to his name.

In some ways it is a more acceptable situation for the state when the prince himself is bad than when his friends are: somehow or other we put up with a single tyrant. For the people can easily satisfy the greed of one man: one man's desires are gratified at no very great expense, and it is possible to quench one man's ferocity. But to satisfy a whole entourage of tyrants is a very heavy burden.

The prince should avoid all innovation as far as proves possible: for even if something is changed for the better, a novel situation is still disturbing in itself.[119] Neither the structure of the state, the customary public business of the city, nor long established laws may be changed without upheaval. Consequently, if something is of a kind that can be tolerated, there is no need for change; the right thing will be either to put up with it or to steer the practice smoothly towards improvement. On the other hand, if something is such that it cannot be tolerated, it will have to be put right—but subtly and gradually.

What general aim the person in power sets himself is of great importance, for if his choice of objective is misguided, then he will necessarily go wrong all the way along. The ultimate intention of the good prince must therefore be not only to guard the present well-being of the state, but also to hand it over in a more flourishing condition than that in which he received it.

However, since good things are of three kinds (to speak in Peripatetic terms), namely spiritual, bodily, and external, he will have to be careful not to take account of them in reverse order and judge the state's welfare mainly by these last 'external' things.[120] For external things must be judged by no other criterion than how

---

[119] In spite of Erasmus's commitment to novelty in learning, he is fundamentally a supporter of the *status quo* in social and political affairs. Hence, in spite of his sympathy with the intellectual arguments, and the criticism of clerical conduct, which provoked Luther to challenge the Catholic Church and its hierarchy, Erasmus insisted that no more was needed than modest internal reforms to current practice, and refused to lend his name to back the Lutheran Reformers.

[120] Aristotle, *Nicomachean Ethics* 1.8.2 and *Politics* 7.1.2.

relevant they are to spiritual and bodily well-being. That is to say, let this be the only way he assesses his people's happiness: not by whether he keeps them in great wealth or in optimal health, but by their honesty and moderation; by the absence of greed, aggressiveness, contention; and by the presence of the fullest possible harmony.

He must take care also on this point, not to be taken in by the false application of fine words. In fact, this is the source from which practically all the world's evils arise and make their advance. For it is not true happiness when a people is given over to idle luxury, nor is it true freedom when people can do what they like. Nor is it servitude to live according to what is prescribed by just laws; nor is it a peaceful state where the people defer to every whim of the prince, but rather when obedience is given to good laws and to a prince whose wise deliberations are consistent with the requirements of the law, And it is not equality for everyone to have the same rewards, the same rights, and the same status; indeed, this often results in extreme inequality.

The prince who is about to take up office must bear this fact especially in mind, that the chief hope for the state is founded in the proper training of its children—something which Xenophon wisely taught in his *Cyropaedia*.[121] For at a tender age they are responsive to any training you like. Consequently the utmost care must be taken over public and private schools and over the education of girls, so that they are straight away in the care of the best and most reliable teachers, where they absorb both Christian principles and also literature that is of sound quality and conducive to the welfare of the state. In this way it will come about that there is truly no need for many laws or penalties, because the citizens follow the right course of their own accord.

Such is the power of education, as Plato has written that a man who has been correctly brought up emerges as a kind of divine creature, while faulty upbringing, on the other hand, reduces him to a horrible monster.[122] And nothing is of greater importance for the prince than that he should have the best possible citizens.

Pains will therefore have to be taken to accustom them from the outset to what is best, for any music sounds sweet to those who

[121] Xenophon, *Cyropaedia* I.2.2–8.
[122] Plato, *Laws* 6.766 A.

have become used to it. And nothing is harder than to withdraw someone from behaviour which has already taken root in his character from habitual usage. But none of these things will prove exceptionally difficult if the prince himself pursues excellence.

It is the mark of the tyrant, indeed an underhand deception, to treat the people at large in the way that animal trainers customarily treat a wild beast; for their prime concern is to observe what pacifies it or what arouses it, and then they provoke or soothe it to suit their own convenience, as Plato has forcibly remarked. For that is not to take popular feeling into consideration but to abuse it.

But if the people are obstinate and resist what is to their own advantage, then either you will have to go along with them for the time being and gradually win them over to your plans, or do this by some skilful strategy or some benign deception. In the same way, when wine is drunk, it yields to the drinker at first until it permeates his veins by degrees and takes the whole person into its power.

And if on occasion the turmoil of affairs and the mood of the people obstruct the prince's plans somewhat and compel him to serve the times, he should still not give in as long as he can keep up the pressure, and what he has not achieved in one way he should try to do in another.

4 *Revenue and taxation*

If we scour the history of the Ancients we shall find that many revolts were occasioned by excessive taxation.[123] Consequently the good prince will have to take care that the feelings of the populace are roused as little as possible on this account. He should rule without cost to the people if he can, for the position of prince is too noble to be commercialised with propriety. And the good prince has in his possession whatever his affectionate subjects possess.

There were many pagans who took nothing back home except glory from the good service they gave to the state. There were one

---

[123] Both More, in his *Utopia*, and Erasmus here held strong views on unjust taxation—a thoroughly topical subject since levies and taxes on subjects were the source of most princely revenue, from secular levies raised in the form of customs charges, poll taxes, monopolies etc., to the indulgences and church taxes raised internationally on behalf of the Pope. On the exceptionally high taxes levied on the Low Countries at the time Erasmus was writing see Tracy, *Politics*, 37–8 and 77–8.

or two, such as Fabius Maximus and Antoninus Pius, who rejected the glory also. How much more ought a Christian prince to be content with the knowledge that he has done what is right, especially since he is in the service of one who does not fail to reward right actions richly?

There are some prince's agents whose only concern is to squeeze as much as possible out of the populace on one fresh pretext after another in the belief that they are properly serving the interests of their princes, as if the latter were the enemies of their people. But let anyone who chooses to pay attention to such men realise that he is a long way from the title of 'prince'.

Rather should his efforts and deliberations be directed to this end, that as little as possible should be exacted from the people. The most welcome way of increasing revenue would be for the prince to abolish superfluous expenditure, to disband redundant offices, to avoid wars and foreign tours (which are very like wars), to check the acquisitiveness of officialdom, and to pay more attention to the just administration of his territory than to its expansion.[124]

Otherwise, if he assesses taxation according to his greed or ambitions, what control or limit will there be in the end? For avarice is boundless, continually goading and putting pressure on what it has set afoot until, as the old proverb has it,[125] the last straw breaks the camel's back and revolution eventually flares up when the people's patience is exhausted—a situation which has put an end to empires which were at one time highly prosperous.[126]

So if necessity requires some taxation of the people, then it is the good prince's job to do it in such a way that the least possible hardship falls on the poor. For it is perhaps politic to summon the

---

[124] These comments are lightly veiled criticisms of the taxation policies of the Habsburg emperor Maximilian, whose empire Charles was to inherit in 1519. 'Foreign tours' may allude to the grant of a huge subsidy by the Estates General of the Netherlands to Prince Charles in February 1516 for his projected journey to Spain; see Tracy, *Politics*, 82. See also Erasmus's comments on Charles's father Philip's ill-fated journeys to England and Spain in the adage 'Spartam nactus es, hanc orna' (II.v.1).

[125] *Adages* I.v.67.

[126] Typically, Erasmus's discussion of taxation is moral—concerned with avoiding excessive hardship, and preserving the good will of the people—without regard for economic arguments.

rich to austerity, but to reduce poor people to hunger and servitude is both very cruel and very risky.

When he is thinking of increasing his retinue, when he is anxious to make a brilliant marriage for his grand-daughter or sister, or to raise all his sons to his own status, or to make his nobles wealthy, or to display his substance to other countries while on foreign tours then the conscientious ruler must continually remind himself how cruel it is that on these accounts so many thousands of men with their wives and children should be starving to death at home, getting into debt, and being driven to complete desperation.[127] For those people who extort from the poor what they basely squander on women and gambling would not count in my judgment even as men, let alone as princes. Yet they do exist (or so rumour has it) and believe that they have the right to behave even in this way.

Indeed the prince should weigh up this further consideration, that it is impossible for a measure ever to be abolished, once it has been introduced to meet some temporary situation, if it seems to be to the financial advantage of the prince or the nobility. When the need for a tax has passed, not only should the people's burden be lifted but as far as possible their expenditure during that previous period should be reimbursed in compensation. Accordingly, someone who is well disposed to his people will beware of establishing an insidious precedent; for if he takes pleasure in the misfortunes of his people or neglects their interests, then he does not amount to a prince whatever his title may be.

Care must be taken meanwhile that discrepancies in wealth are not excessive: not that I would want anyone to be forcibly deprived of his goods, but some system should be operated to prevent the wealth of the many from being allocated to the few. Plato, for one, wants his citizens to be neither too rich nor on the other hand particularly poor, since the poor man is unable to make a social contribution while the rich man is unwilling to do so by using his own talents.[128]

How is it that princes quite often do not even get rich from taxes of this sort? Anyone who wants to understand this may reflect on

---

[127] This passage reads like a direct comment on the activities of Maximilian.
[128] Plato, *Republic* 4.421 D; see also Aristotle, *Politics* 4.9.4–5. Unlike More, Erasmus does not suggest that abolishing private property might be an effective way of avoiding the social strains of differential wealth.

how much less our ancestors received from their subjects, and yet how much more generous they were and how much more profusely they were supplied with all things; the reason is that the best part of the revenue now slips through the fingers of these gatherers and receivers, mentioned above, and only a tiny part reaches the prince himself.[129]

The good prince will therefore impose as little tax as possible on those things whose use is shared also by the poorest ranks of the people, such as corn, bread, beer, wine, clothes, and all the other things without which human life cannot be carried on.[130] But these things at present carry a very heavy burden, and in more than one way: first by the very heavy taxes which the revenue agents extort (and which the people call 'assizes'), then by import duties, which even have their own agents to themselves, and lastly by the monopolies. In order that a very little income may get back to the prince from these sources, the poorer people are milked dry by this expenditure.

Much the best way, therefore, of increasing the value of the prince's income, as has been said, is to reduce his outgoing costs, and even in his case the proverb holds good that thrift is a great source of revenue. But if it is unavoidable that some levy be made, and the people's interests demand such action, then let the burden fall on those foreign and imported goods which are not so much necessities of life as luxurious and pleasurable refinements and whose use is confined to the rich, such as cotton, silk, dyed cloth, pepper, spices, ointments, jewels, and anything else of this kind. For in this way the inconvenience will be felt only by those who have the good fortune to be able to bear it; and the expense will not render them destitute but will perhaps make them less extravagant, so that what they lose in money is made good to them in a moral benefit.[131]

---

[129] Another topical observation concerning the phenomenal wealth being accumulated by merchant banking houses like the German Fuggers who collected taxes on behalf of popes and princes.

[130] For a more detailed denunciation of such taxes see the adage 'A mortuo tributum exigere' (I.ix.12).

[131] Like most liberal thinkers on taxation in the period (including More), Erasmus here advocates the levying of revenue on luxury imported goods, rather than on necessities and goods manufactured at home.

In the coinage of money the good prince will display the trust-worthiness he owes both to God and to the people, and will not allow himself to do things for which he punishes other people most harshly. The people are commonly robbed in four ways over this business, as we saw for some considerable time after the death of Charles,[132] when a kind of protracted anarchy more dangerous than tyranny afflicted your kingdom: first, when the material for the coinage is contaminated by some sort of alloy; secondly, when it is underweight; next, when it is reduced by clipping round the edge; lastly, when it is constantly being devalued and revalued whenever it is seen to be to the advantage of the royal treasury.[133]

5 Generosity in the prince

If kindliness and generosity are the special glory of good princes, how can certain people lay claim to the title of prince when their whole policy is directed towards fostering their own interests at the expense of everyone else? The skilful and vigilant prince will there-fore seek ways of helping everyone, and that does not mean simply by handing out gifts. He will assist some by his liberality and raise up others by his support; he will use his authority to restore those who are cast down and his advice to help others. In fact, he will be inclined to regard as wasted any day in which he has not used his power for good to help someone.

The prince's bounty must not be distributed recklessly, however. Some extort ruthlessly from good citizens what they squander on jesters, informers, and those who minister to their pleasures. The state should be aware that the prince will most often show kindness towards those who work hardest for the common good. Generosity should be the reward of virtue, not the result of a whim.

---

[132] Charles the Bold, Duke of Burgundy, and great-grandfather of Prince Charles. For Erasmus's low opinion of him see the adage 'Spartam nactus es, hanc orna' (II.v.1). Charles died in battle in 1477, leaving no male heir. This led to a pro-longed struggle over the inheritance between France and the house of Austria, and the attendant economic upheavals (devaluation and revaluation of currency to finance military campaigns).

[133] Erasmus and More are also in agreement on the negative effects of manipulation of the value of coin by the prince and his administration. See *Utopia* I.

The prince must try especially to practise the sort of generosity that involves no disadvantage, or at least no harm, to anyone else. Robbing one group to enrich another, ruining some to advance others: far from being services, such actions are disservices twice over, particularly if what has been taken from worthy men is turned over to the unworthy.

Not for nothing do the myths of the poets tell us how the gods never visited a place without conferring some great benefit on those who received them. But if, at the approach of their prince, his citizens hide any elegant furniture, lock up their pretty daughters, send away their young sons, conceal their wealth, and do all they can to make themselves inconspicuous: is it not obvious what they think of him, since they act exactly as they would at the approach of an enemy or a robber? Since on their prince's arrival they fear for all the things it should be his duty to protect against the threat of treachery or violence? They fear treachery from the others, but they fear violence too from him: one man complains that he has been beaten up, another that his daughter has been abducted, another that his wife has been raped, and yet another that some trifling payment has been withheld. What a difference, indeed, between this prince's arrival and those descriptions of the gods! The more prosperous a city the more it suspects the prince, and on the prince's arrival all the more disreputable elements rush out, whereas all the best and wisest citizens are put on their guard and keep themselves to themselves; even if they say nothing, their actions proclaim their opinion of the prince. Someone may reply to this: 'I cannot keep a check on the activities of all my followers; I am doing my best.' Make your followers understand that you really have your heart set on this course, and I shall be very surprised if that will not keep them in check. In the end, you will convince the people that such crimes are committed against your will only if you do not allow them to go unpunished.

It was perhaps sufficient for a pagan prince to be generous towards his own citizens, but merely just towards foreigners. But it is the mark of a Christian prince to consider no one a foreigner except those who are strangers to the sacraments of Christ, and to avoid provoking even these by doing them injury. Of course he must fulfil his obligations towards his own citizens first, but for the rest, as far as possible, he should help all men.

Although it should be the prince's constant concern to protect everyone from harm, yet, as Plato suggests, he should make more diligent efforts to prevent harm befalling visitors than his own citizens, because visitors, bereft of the support of friends and relations, are more exposed to danger; for this reason they were thought to be under Jupiter's protection, and gave him the name *Xenios*.

6 Enacting or amending laws

The principal method of making a city or kingdom prosperous is to have the best of laws under the best of princes; the happiest situation arises when the prince is obeyed by all and himself obeys the laws, provided that these conform to the ideals of justice and honour and have no other purpose than to advance the interests of all.[134]

The good, wise, and upright prince is simply a sort of embodiment of the law.[135] He will therefore spare no effort to enact the best possible laws, those most beneficial to the state, rather than a great number. A very small number of laws will be sufficient in a well-ordered state under a good prince and honest magistrates, and if things are otherwise, no amount of laws will suffice. When an incompetent doctor tries one remedy after another, his patients tend to suffer.

In enacting laws, special care must be taken to ensure that they do not smell of profit for the privy purse or of special treatment for the nobility; everything should be related to an ideal standard of honour and to the public interest, and this should be defined, not by the opinion of the mob, but according to the precepts of wisdom, which should always be present at the councils of princes; in other words, as the pagans also agree, there will be no true law unless it is just, fair, and conducive to the common good. Nor does something become law simply because the prince has so decided, unless the decision is that of a wise and good prince, who will decide on

---

[134] The ideal state of affairs, according to Erasmus, is one in which there is a perfect identity between that order the prince supports, that which is best for the people as a whole, and the law of the land.

[135] See Aristotle, *Politics* 3.8.2, Cicero, *Laws* 3.1.2, and Plutarch, *Moralia* 780 C–E. This is a crucial argument for Erasmus's theory of education for the Christian prince. It makes the prince ethically synonymous with the law of his land.

nothing that is not honourable and in the best interests of the state. If the standards by which wrongdoing is to be judged are themselves distorted, the only result will be that even things that were just will be perverted by laws of this kind.

Plato too requires as few laws as possible, especially on less important subjects such as contracts, business deals, and taxation.[136] For, he says, the state is not made healthy by a great number of laws any more than a man by a great number of medicines. Where the prince is impartial and the magistrates do their job, there is no need for many laws; where things are otherwise, abuse of the laws will lead the state to perdition, and the dishonesty of these men will divert even laws properly enacted to other purposes.

The tyrannical scheme of Dionysius of Syracuse has been justly censured; he passed a great many laws, piling one on top of another, but he is said to have allowed his people to ignore them and in this way to have made everyone beholden to him. That was not making laws, but setting traps.

Epitades too has been deservedly condemned for passing a law whereby a man was free to leave his property to anyone he liked; but he only did this so that he could disinherit his own son whom he hated. At first the people did not see through the man's trick, but in the end the affair brought the state to the brink of disaster.

The prince should promote the kind of laws which not only prescribe punishment for the guilty but also dissuade men from breaking the law. It is thus a mistake to think that the laws should be restricted to the shortest possible form of words, so that they merely give orders and not instruction; on the contrary, they should be concerned to deter men from law-breaking more by reasoning than by punishments. As it happens, Seneca disagrees with Plato's opinion here, but in doing so he shows more boldness than wisdom.[137]

Again, Plato does not allow young men to debate the fairness of a law, although he allows this to their elders, in moderation.[138] But if it is not the people's role to voice ill-considered opinions of the prince's laws, it is the prince's duty to ensure that his laws will be

---

[136] Plato, *Republic* 4.425 C–E. More's *Utopia* also has few laws, thereby avoiding the proliferation of interpretations of the law which bogs down administration.

[137] Seneca, *Epistulae morales* 94.38; in fact, Seneca is quoting Posidonius' disapproval of Plato's opinion—Seneca himself clearly agrees with Plato.

[138] Plato, *Laws* 1.634 D–E.

acceptable to all good men, remembering that even the humblest of men have a certain common sense. Antoninus Pius has been praised because he never proposed anything without attempting to justify it to everyone by edicts in which he gave his reasons for judging it useful to the state.

In his *Oeconomicus*, Xenophon shrewdly demonstrated that all other creatures can be made to obey by two things in particular: inducements, such as food, if they are of the lower sort, or caresses, if they are nobler, like the horse; or blows, if they are stubborn, like the ass. But since man is the noblest of all creatures, it is only fitting that he should be induced to observe the law by rewards, rather than coerced by threats and punishment.[139]

Therefore the law should not only prescribe penalties for wrong-doers but also provide rewards to encourage service to the state. We know that the Ancients had many laws of this kind: anyone who had distinguished himself in battle could hope for a reward, and if he fell, his children were brought up at public expense; anyone who had rescued a citizen, thrown down an enemy from the walls, or assisted the state with sound advice was entitled to a reward.

Of course the better sort of citizen will always follow the best course even if no reward is offered, but these inducements are useful to inspire the less well educated to pursue an honourable course.

Men of noble character are more interested in honour; the baser sort are attracted by money too. Thus a law will make use of all these methods to influence men: honour and disgrace, profit and loss. Finally, men of thoroughly servile, or rather bestial, disposition must be tamed by chains and the lash.

Citizens should be familiar with this sense of honour and disgrace from boyhood onwards, so that they know that rewards are given for good conduct rather than for wealth or connections.

In short, the vigilant prince should direct his best efforts, not simply to punishing crime, but to looking beyond that, and taking pains to ensure that no crime worthy of punishment is committed in the first place.[140]

A doctor who prevents disease and keeps it away is better than one who expels it with medicine once it is established. Similarly, it

[139] Xenophon, *Oeconomicus* 13.6–10.
[140] Here, as throughout this section, More and Erasmus are very much of a mind.

81

is far better to ensure that no offences at all are committed than to punish them once they have been perpetrated. This will be achieved if the prince can destroy, if possible, or at least check and reduce anything that he has noted as a likely source of criminal behaviour.

First, as we have said, the vast majority of crimes spring, as if from a muddy fountain, from perverted ideas about the state of things. Your first aim therefore should be to have citizens in whom the best of principles have been implanted, and your second, that the magistrates should be not only wise but uncorrupted.

Plato rightly warns that everything else must be tried, that no stone, as they say, should be left unturned, before the supreme penalty is invoked.[141] To persuade men not to break the law, you must first use reasoned arguments, then, as a deterrent, the fear of divine vengeance against criminals, and in addition threats of punishment. If these are ineffective, you must resort to punishment, but of a comparatively light kind, more to cure the disease than to kill the patient. If none of this is successful, then at last the law must reluctantly cut the criminal off, like a hopeless, incurable limb, to prevent the infection spreading to the healthy part.

A reliable and skilful doctor will not resort to amputation or cauterisation if he can cure the disease by compresses or a draught of medicine, and will never fall back on them unless compelled by the illness to do so. In the same way, the prince will try all other remedies before resorting to capital punishment, remembering that the state is one body; no one cuts off a limb if it can be restored to health in some other way.

In applying his treatment, the conscientious doctor concentrates on getting rid of the illness with the minimum of danger to his patient; similarly, in framing his laws, the good prince will consider nothing but the public interest and seek to remedy the ills of the people with the minimum of discomfort.

A good many crimes arise particularly from the fact that in every country riches are prized and poverty is scorned. The prince will therefore strive to ensure that his subjects are respected for good conduct and good character rather than for wealth, and he should apply this first to himself and his court. If the people see the prince flaunting his wealth, if they see that at his court the richest men are the most admired and that the road to the magistracy, honours, and

---

[141] Plato, *Laws* 9.862 E.

public office is open to cash, then of course all this will incite the common people to acquire wealth by fair means or foul.

Now, to speak more generally, many of the pitfalls which exist in every state are the result of idleness, which everyone seeks in different ways. Once men have acquired a taste for it, they turn to the paths of evil if they lack the means to provide for it. The vigilant prince will therefore ensure that he has as few idlers as possible among his subjects, either making them work or banishing them from the state.

Plato thinks that all beggars must be driven out of his republic. But if there are men broken by illness or old age, with no family to care for them, they should be looked after in state institutions for the old and the sick.[142] A man who is in good health and satisfied with little will not need to beg.

The inhabitants of Marseilles refused entry to some priests who, in order to live in idleness and luxury under the guise of religion, used to hawk certain sacred relics from town to town. Perhaps, too, it would be to the state's advantage to limit the number of monasteries. For monastic life too is a kind of idleness, especially for those whose lives have been far from blameless and who now fritter away lethargic lives in idleness. My remarks about monasteries apply to colleges as well.[143]

Under this heading too come tax farmers, pedlars, usurers, brokers, panders, estate managers, game wardens, the whole gang of agents and retainers whom some people keep purely for the sake of ostentation. When men like these cannot meet the demands of extravagance, the concomitant of idleness, they lapse into evil ways.

Soldiering, too, is a very energetic kind of idleness, and much the most dangerous, since it causes the total destruction of everything worthwhile and opens up a cesspit of everything that is evil. And so, if the prince will banish from his realm all such seed-beds of crime, there will be much less for his laws to punish.

Thus useful occupations must be held in high esteem and, I should add in passing, ineffective idleness should not go under the name of nobility. I would not wish to strip their honours from those

---

[142] Plato, *Laws* 11.936 c.

[143] Here Erasmus is pointedly critical of two institutions of which he personally had practical experience. Wherever he shifts his attention from moral precepts to social criticism his views closely match those expressed in similar language in More's *Utopia* (II.128, 35 sqq).

of noble birth, if they upheld the standards of their forebears and excelled in those activities which originally created the aristocracy. But when we see so many of them these days grown soft with idleness, emasculated by their debauches, devoid of any useful talent, little more than jolly table-companions and devoted gamblers—I pass over their more revolting activities—why on earth should this sort of fellow be treated better than a cobbler or a farmer? In days gone by the aristocracy were excused the more menial tasks, not to allow them to waste time, but to learn those skills which help in the government of the state.

Therefore, rich or noble citizens should not be frowned on for instructing their sons in some sedentary occupation; for one thing, young men preoccupied with their studies will be kept away from many temptations, and for another, even if they have no need of their skills at least they harm no one. But, since human affairs are subject to the vagaries of fortune if the need arises then skill will find its reward, not only in any land, as the proverb says, but in any station in life too.[144]

The Ancients, recognising that many problems arise from extravagance and luxurious living, counteracted them by sumptuary laws and appointed inspectors to control excessive expenditure on banquets, clothes, or buildings. If anyone thinks it harsh to prevent a man from using or abusing his own property as he pleases, let him reflect that it is much harsher to let social standards deteriorate, through luxurious living, to the point where capital punishment is required, and that it is less harsh to be compelled to live frugally than to be brought to perdition by vice.

There is nothing more harmful than for magistrates to make a profit out of convicting citizens. Who will exert himself to keep crime down to a minimum, if it is in his interest that there should be as many criminals as possible?

It is appropriate, and it was the custom among the Ancients, that money from fines should go primarily to the injured party, some part of it to public funds and, in the case of the most odious crimes, something also to the informer. But the degree of odiousness must be decided, not by the personal feelings of any one man, but according to the damage or benefit to the state.

---

[144] *Adages* I.vii.33: 'Artem quaevis alit terra'.

The whole purpose of the law should be to protect everyone, rich or poor, noble or humble, serf or free man, public official or private citizen. But it should incline more towards helping the weaker elements, because the position of humble men exposes them more easily to danger. The law's indulgence should compensate for the privileges denied them by their station in life. There should thus be more severe punishment for a crime against a poor man than for offences against the rich, for a corrupt official than for a common criminal, and for a wicked nobleman than for a humble citizen.[145]

According to Plato, there are two kinds of penalty. For the first, care must be taken that the punishment is not too harsh for the crime, and for this reason the supreme penalty must not be invoked lightly; nor must the gravity of the crime be measured by our greed, but fairly and honourably. Why is it that, contrary to the laws of all the Ancients, simple theft is generally punished by death, while adultery goes virtually unpunished? Is it that everyone values money too highly, and so its loss is judged, not on the facts, but on emotional grounds? But this is not the place to discuss why adulterers, on whom the laws used to be very severe, are less severely treated today.

The other kind of penalty, which Plato calls exemplary, must be invoked very sparingly; it should act as a deterrent to others more by its rarity than by its frightfulness. For there is nothing so horrifying that familiarity does not breed contempt for it, nor anything so harmful as allowing one's subjects to become inured to a punishment.[146]

Just as new remedies should not be tried out on a disease if the old ones will cure the illness, so new laws should not be enacted if the old ones will provide a means to treat the ills of the state.

If useless laws cannot be repealed without much trouble, they should be allowed gradually to lapse or else be amended. It is dangerous to alter laws without due consideration, but it is also necessary to adapt the law to the present circumstances of the state, just as treatment is adapted to suit the condition of the patient: some laws, appropriate enough when enacted, are still more appropriately repealed.

---

[145] Erasmus's position on the law here is very much that of the moralist rather than the politician.

[146] Plato, *Laws* 9.854.

Many laws have been introduced quite justifiably but have been put to the worst uses by the corruption of officials; there is nothing so pernicious as a good law diverted to evil purposes. The prince must not be deterred from removing or amending such laws by any loss of revenue, for there is no profit to be made from the loss of honour, especially since the repeal of this kind of law will be much applauded. Nor should the prince be deceived by the fact that laws of this kind have grown up almost everywhere and are now firmly established by long custom; justice, essentially, is not a matter of mere numbers, and the more deeply rooted an evil practice the more thoroughly it needs to be extirpated.

Here are a few examples. In some places it is the practice that a prefect takes possession, in the king's name, of the property of anyone who dies while abroad. This was introduced, quite rightly, to prevent the property of a traveller being claimed by people who had no right to it; it remained in the hands of the prefect for a short time, until the true heirs came forward. But now the custom has been most unjustly perverted, so that whether the heir comes forward or not the traveller's property goes into the prince's treasury.

A law was rightly introduced to allow property found in the possession of a thief when arrested to be seized by the prince or by an officer in his name; obviously this was to prevent property going to the wrong person by some trick, if everyone had the right to claim. As soon as ownership was established, the property would be restored. But now anything found in a thief's possession is regarded by some princes as their own, as if it were part of their patrimony. They are well aware that this practice is shamefully unjust, but the profit motive overcomes honourable intentions.

It was a good idea, in days gone by, to provide officials on the frontiers of states to supervise imports and exports, to ensure, of course, that merchants and travellers could come and go free from the fear of bandits. If anything was stolen, each prince would ensure, within the boundaries of his realm, that the merchants should not suffer any loss and the robber not go unpunished; later, perhaps as a courtesy, merchants began to pay a small fee. But nowadays the traveller is held up at every turn by these customs duties, visitors are harassed, merchants are fleeced, and there is no longer any word of protecting them although the tolls increase from one day to the next. In this way the purpose for which the institution was first established has been totally lost, and what was a sound practice when introduced has been turned into utter tyranny by the fault of those who administer it.[147]

It was established in days gone by that property washed ashore from a shipwreck should be held by the prefect of the sea, not so that it should pass into his hands or the prince's but so that they could prevent it being seized by the wrong people; it would finally become public property if no one survived with a rightful claim on it. But today, in some places, anything which falls into the sea, no matter how, is taken as his own by the prefect, who is more merciless than the sea itself: for anything which the storm has left to the miserable survivors he snatches away like a second storm.[148]

You can see, then, how everything has gone wrong. The thief is punished for seizing another's property; but the magistrate, appointed to prevent theft, does the same, and the rightful owner is robbed twice over by the very man employed to spare him such loss. Merchants too are much harassed and robbed by those appointed specifically to prevent travellers being harassed and robbed. Property is withheld from its rightful owner by the very man appointed by law to prevent it getting into the wrong hands. In many lands there is a vast number of similar institutions, no less unjust than injustice itself. But it is not my purpose in this treatise to reproach any particular state, since these things are common to practically all—and are condemned by them all; I have listed them for the sake of instruction. It may be true that some of them cannot be abrogated without a great upheaval, but their abrogation will win the prince approval and—something more important than any financial gain—a good reputation.

Like the prince, the law must, more than anything else, be accessible and fair to all; otherwise, as the Greek philosopher cleverly put it, the laws will be nothing but spiders' webs, which birds can easily

---

[147] Several of these examples of legal practice which once had an equitable purpose, but is now used to extort revenue for the crown, are ones in which Erasmus, with his itinerant life-style, was directly interested. He risked dying outside his native land, and he risked not being able to retrieve property stolen from him (he lost money and goods on a number of occasions). On Erasmus's unfortunate experience at the hands of English customs at Dover see ep. 119 (and see the adage 'A mortuo tributum exigere' (i.ix.12)).

[148] Erasmus may have in mind here a scandalous incident of this kind which took place in the Netherlands in 1516. See Preserved Smith, *Colloquies*, 18–20.

break because of their size, and in which only flies will be entangled.[149]

Like the prince, the law must always be more willing to forgive than to punish, either because it has a certain intrinsic mildness, or because it is a reflection of the ways of God, slow to be moved to anger and vengeance, or, again, because a man wrongly released can be recalled for punishment, but a man unjustly condemned cannot be helped; even if he is still alive, who can put a price on another man's suffering?[150]

We read that in days gone by there was a kind of men, tyrants, not princes—and the conduct of the Christian prince must be entirely different—for whom the measure of a crime was the harm done to their personal interests; so they thought it mere petty theft to strip a pauper of his property and condemn him, with his wife and children, to slavery or to beggary, but a most serious theft, worthy of the sternest punishment, to cheat the privy purse or some rapacious official even of a few coins. Again, they would cry *lèse majesté*[151] if anyone murmured against a prince, however bad, or spoke a little too freely of some pestilent magistrate. But the pagan emperor Hadrian, not normally included among good princes, never allowed a charge of *lèse majesté*, and not even the ruthless Nero set much store by accusations of this sort. Another one, who completely ignored charges of this kind, is supposed to have said: 'In a free state, tongues too should be free.'

It follows that the good prince will forgive no offences more easily and willingly than those which damage his personal interests: who will find it easier to overlook such things than the prince? The easier vengeance may be, the more it will appear invidious and unseemly, since vengeance is the mark of a weak and mean spirit, and nothing is less appropriate to the prince, whose spirit must be lofty and magnanimous.

It is not enough for the prince to keep clear of crime unless he is also free from any suspicion or taint of crime. For this reason he

---

[149] See *Adages* I.iv.47.

[150] Erasmus's insistence that the law is in all things as morally exemplary as the prince derives directly from his statement that the good prince and his laws are one.

[151] The crime of *maiestas minuta*—'treason'—was originally an offence against the majesty of the Roman people; under the empire its scope was broadened to take account of the existence of the prince.

will consider not only the deserts of the man who has committed a crime against him, but also how other men will judge the prince, and he will sometimes show mercy in an undeserving case out of concern for his honour, and pardon a man unworthy of pardon to safeguard his reputation.

Let no one immediately cry out that this advice takes too little account of the majesty of a prince, which it should be the state's principal concern to keep sacrosanct and inviolate. On the contrary, there is no better safeguard for his greatness than that the people know him to be so vigilant that nothing escapes him, so wise that he understands the true sources of the prince's majesty, and so merciful that he will avenge no offence against himself unless the public interest demands it. The pardon granted to Cinna made the majesty of Augustus Caesar both more glorious and more secure, when so many executions had had no effect.

Lèse majesté occurs only when a man has diminished those qualities which make the prince truly great; if his greatness lies in the excellence of his mind and the prosperity which his wisdom brings to his people, then anyone who undermines these must be accused of *lèse majesté*. It is a great mistake, and a complete misunderstanding of the true majesty of the prince, to suppose that this can be increased if the law and public liberties are little respected, as if prince and state were two separate entities. If a comparison must be made between things which nature has united, a king should not compare himself with any one of his subjects but with the whole body of the state: then he will realise that the latter, comprising so many distinguished men and women, is worth far more than the head alone, the prince.[152] A state, even if it lacks a prince, will still be a state. Vast empires have flourished without a prince, such as Rome and Athens under democracy. But a prince simply cannot exist without a state, and in fact the state takes in the prince, rather than the reverse. What makes a prince a great man, except the consent of his subjects?[153] On the other hand, if a man achieves

---

[152] Once again Erasmus insists that the prince is bound to observe those laws which benefit his entire people, rather than enacting laws for his own benefit.

[153] A clear statement of Erasmus's fundamental position. A prince is not necessary to a state, which can establish the rule of law on behalf of its people by democratic republican rule. The rule of a prince depends on his subjects' agreeing thus to be ruled.

greatness by goodness, that is, by his virtues, he will still be a great man even if deprived of his power.

It is obvious, therefore, that those who measure a prince's honour by standards unworthy of a prince's grandeur are quite wrong in their judgment. They call traitor (a word supposed by them to be the most loathsome of all) a man who, by advice freely given, recalls his prince to better paths when he strays and puts at risk his honour, his safety, and his country's welfare. But a man who corrupts the prince with ignoble ideas and launches him into a round of sordid pleasures, feasts, gambling, and similar indignities: surely such a man is not preserving the prince's honour? They call it loyalty to humour a foolish prince with constant flattery, and treason to oppose his shameful enterprises. But no one is less a friend to the prince than a man who deludes him and leads him astray by base flattery, who involves him in wars, advises him to pillage the people, teaches him the arts of the tyrant, and causes him to be hated by all decent people; this is real treason, and deserves no mean punishment.

Plato requires that the 'guardians of the law', that is, those appointed to watch over the laws, be the least corruptible of men.[154] The good prince should never act more severely than against those who administer the law corruptly, since the prince himself is the chief of the 'guardians of the law'.

To sum up: it is best to have as few laws as possible; these should be as just as possible and further the public interest; they should also be as familiar as possible to the people: for this reason the Ancients exhibited them in tables and on tablets in public places for all to see. It is disgraceful that certain men use the laws like a spider's web, plainly intending to entangle as many as possible, not in the interest of the state, but simply to catch their prey. Finally, the laws should be drafted in plain terms, with the minimum of complications, so that there is little need for that grasping sort who call themselves lawyers and advocates; once, in fact, this profession was the preserve of the best men in society, bringing little profit but much honour; but nowadays the profit motive has corrupted it, as it vitiates everything.

[154] Plato, *Laws* 6.755 A.

Plato says that there is no enemy more dangerous to the state than the man who subjects the laws to human eccentricity, whereas under the best princes the laws will possess supreme authority.[155]

7 Magistrates[156] and their duties

The prince must demand from his officials the same standards of integrity, or very nearly, as he himself exhibits. He should not think it enough simply to have appointed magistrates; the manner of their appointment is of the greatest importance, and he must then see to it that they carry out scrupulously their appointed tasks.

Aristotle made the important and judicious observation that it is useless to establish good laws if there is no one who will labour to uphold what has been so well established; indeed, it sometimes happens that the best established laws are turned to the total ruin of the state through the fault of the magistrates.[157]

Although magistrates must not be chosen for their wealth, their pedigree, or their age, but rather for their wisdom and integrity, yet it is better to appoint older men to this kind of post, on which the well-being of the state depends, not only because old men have acquired prudence with experience and are more temperate in their appetites, but also because their advancing years confer on them a kind of authority in the minds of the people. For this reason Plato forbids the appointment of men younger than fifty or older than seventy as guardians of the laws.[158] He would not have a priest younger than sixty. Just as there is a certain point in life when a man reaches maturity, so there is a certain decline in life which requires retirement and a rest from all duties.

A choral dance makes an elegant spectacle so long as it is performed with order and harmony, but it becomes farcical if the gestures and voices get confused; similarly, a kingdom or city is an excellent institution if everyone is assigned a place and performs his proper function, that is, if the prince acts like a prince, the magis-

---

[155] Plato, *Laws* 3.690.
[156] Erasmus means by 'magistrate' any senior government administrator or officer of state, not merely officers of the law.
[157] Aristotle, *Politics* 4.6.3.
[158] Plato, *Laws* 6.755 A.

trates play their parts, and the people submit to good laws and upright magistrates. But where the prince acts in his own interest and the magistrates simply plunder the people, where the people do not submit to honourable laws but flatter prince and magistrates, whatever they do—there, the most appalling confusion must reign.

The first and chief concern of the prince must be to serve the state to the best of his ability: he can do it no greater service than to ensure that the magistrature and its duties are entrusted to the most upright men, those most devoted to the common good.

What is the prince but a physician to the state? But it is not enough for a physician to have skilful assistants; he must himself be the most skilful and careful of all. Similarly, it is not enough for the prince to have virtuous magistrates; he must himself be the most virtuous of all, since it is he who chooses and corrects them.

The parts of the mind are not all equals: some give instructions, others carry them out, while the body does no more than carry out instructions. In the same way the prince, the highest part of the state, must be the most discerning, and entirely free from all gross passions. Next to him stand the magistrates, partly carrying out and partly giving instructions; they obey the prince but command the people.

Thus the happiness of the state depends particularly on its magistrates being impartially appointed and impartially performing their duties. There should therefore be provisions against maladministration, just as the Ancients had them against extortion. Finally, if they are convicted, the most severe punishment should be decreed against them.

They will be appointed impartially if the prince nominates, not the highest bidder, the most brazen lobbyist, his closest relatives, or those most adept at pandering to his character, passions, and desires, but rather those most upright in character and best suited to perform the appointed tasks.

Otherwise, when a prince merely sells appointments for the best price he can get, what else can he expect but that his appointees will resell them, making good their own outlay as best they can, and trading on their office, since they acquired it by a business deal?[159] This practice should not be thought any the less dangerous to the

[159] Selling offices was a source of revenue for the state in most European countries.

state just because, by long and wretched usage, it has won acceptance with a number of nations, since it was frowned on even by the pagans, and the laws of the Caesars lay down that those who preside over the courts must be given the inducement of a princely salary so that they have no excuse for graft.

In days gone by, the charge of giving a corrupt verdict was treated very seriously; but on what grounds can a prince punish a judge for taking bribes to give or withhold a verdict, if the prince himself has sold off the job of making judgments and was in fact the first to instruct the judge in the ways of corruption? Let the prince treat the magistrates as he would have them treat the people.

In the *Politics*, Aristotle wisely remarks that, above all, care must be taken that magistrates do not make money out of their duties; otherwise, two disadvantages occur: first, it will mean that the magistracy will be sought after, or should I say be attacked and overwhelmed, by the most grasping and corrupt of men, and, second, the people will suffer the double blow of being excluded from office and robbed of their money.[160]

8 Treaties

In making treaties, as in everything else, the good prince will pursue only the public interest. Otherwise, if they are arranged to benefit the princes at the expense of the people, they should be called conspiracies, not treaties. Anyone who acts like this makes one people into two, nobility and commons, and one of them profits only from the other's loss; but where this happens, there is no state.[161]

There is a most binding and holy contract between all Christian princes, simply from the fact that they are Christians. What, then, is the point of negotiating treaties day after day, as if everyone were the enemy of everyone else, as if human contracts could achieve what Christ cannot?[162] When business is done by means of a lot of

---

[160] Aristotle, *Politics* 5.7.9.

[161] More was as sceptical as Erasmus about the benefit of treaties to the state. Unlike Erasmus he had a good deal of first-hand experience of negotiating such treaties.

[162] Erasmus must have been aware that this simplistic view of the inevitable good faith and trust between Christian princes was directly contradicted by contemporary political manœuvrings among the major powers—which included secret treaty negotiations between Christian princes and the Muslim Ottomans.

bits of paper, it suggests that there is little trust present, and we often see that a great deal of litigation arises from the very things that were supposed to preclude litigation. Where mutual trust exists and business is being done between honest men, there is no need for a lot of these niggling bits of paper, but when business is being done between dishonest and untrustworthy men the bits of paper actually provide raw material for the courts. Similarly, friendship will exist between good and wise princes even if there is no treaty between them, but war will arise between bad and foolish princes out of the very treaties designed to prevent war, when one of them complains that one or other of the innumerable clauses has not been observed. Treaties are supposed to be made to put an end to war, but nowadays an agreement to start war is called a treaty. Alliances of this kind are no more than stratagems of war, and as the situation develops, the treaties fall into line with it.

The good faith of princes in fulfilling their agreements must be such that a simple promise from them will be more sacred than any oath sworn by other men. How shameful it is, then, to fail to fulfil the conditions of a solemn treaty, one sworn by those things which Christians hold most sacred! Yet every day we can see this becoming the custom; I will not say who is at fault, but it certainly could not happen unless someone is at fault.

If some clause of a treaty has apparently not been observed, this must not be taken at once as evidence that the treaty as a whole is null and void, because this will suggest that a pretext has been found for breaking off friendly relations. On the contrary, great efforts should be made to repair the breach with as little damage as possible; indeed the best course sometimes is to connive at something like this, since even an understanding between private citizens will not hold together for long if they take everything, as it were, too literally.[163] Do not immediately follow the course dictated by anger, but rather that suggested by the public interest.

The good and wise prince will try to be at peace with all nations but particularly with his neighbours, who can do much harm if they are hostile and much good if they are friendly; no state can survive for long without good relations with them. In addition, it is easy for friendship to be made and kept between those who are linked

---

[163] *Adages* II.iv.13, 'Ad vivum resecare'.

by a common language, by the proximity of their lands, and by similarities of temperament and character.[164] Certain nations are so different from one another in every way that it would be advisable to refrain from any contact with them rather than be linked to them even by the most binding of treaties. Others are so distant that even if they are well disposed they can be of no help. There are others, finally, who are so capricious, so insolent, such habitual breakers of treaties, that even if they are neighbours they are useless as friends. With this sort the best plan is neither to break with them by open war nor to be linked to them by any very binding treaties or marriage alliances, because war is always disastrous, and certain people's friendship is not much better than war.

One element of wise government will therefore be a knowledge of the character and temperament of all races, gathered partly from books and partly from the accounts of wise and well-travelled men; do not imagine that, with Ulysses, you must travel across all lands and seas. Beyond this, it may not be easy to lay down hard and fast rules. One may state as a general rule that it is not advisable to be too closely allied with those, such as the heathen, who are divided from us by a difference of religion, and we should neither encourage nor reject those whom natural obstacles, such as mountain barriers or seas, separate from us, or those who are totally cut off from us by vast distances. There are many examples of this, but one will suffice for all, since it is closest at hand: the kingdom of France is by far and in every way the most prosperous of all; but she would have been still more prosperous had she refrained from invading Italy.[165]

9 *The marriage alliances of princes*

In my judgment it would be most beneficial to the state if the marriage alliances of princes were confined within the boundaries of their kingdom; if they must go beyond their frontiers, they should

---

[164] In the adage, 'Spartam nactus es, hanc orna' (II.v.1) Erasmus gives the example of the impossibility of any lasting alliance between the Spanish and the Germans. Since Prince Charles stood to inherit both territories the example is omitted here.

[165] In the adage 'Spartum nactus es, hanc orna' (II.v.1) Erasmus deplores the efforts of the French kings Charles VIII and Louis XII to invade Italy, which had been going on since 1494.

be united only with near neighbours and then only with those best suited to a pact of friendship.[166] But, people will say, it is unseemly for the daughter of a king to be joined with any but a king or a king's son. But bettering one's family whenever possible is an ambition for private citizens, and the prince must be as different as possible from them. What does it matter if a prince's sister marries a man less powerful than he, if it is for the greater good of all? A prince will win more honour by disregarding rank in his sister's marriage than by putting the whim of a mere woman before the public interest.

To a certain extent the marriage of princes is a private affair, but we must acknowledge that sometimes the whole course of events may come to depend almost entirely on this one point, so that what happened long ago to the Greeks and Trojans over Helen often happens to us. If a choice worthy of the prince is to be made, let a woman be chosen who is distinguished among her fellows by her honesty, modesty, and prudence, who will make an obedient wife for the best of princes, and will bear him children worthy of both parents and of their country. Whatever her parentage, she will be noble enough if she makes a good wife for a good prince.

It is generally agreed that nothing is so beneficial to everyone as that the prince should warmly love his people and be loved by them in return. In this area a common fatherland, similar characteristics of body and mind, and a sort of national aura arising from some secret affinity of temperament are of enormous importance, but most of this is bound to disappear if it is disturbed by the wrong sort of marriage. It is hardly likely that children born of such a marriage will be accepted wholeheartedly by the country, nor will they themselves be wholeheartedly devoted to the country.[167]

---

[166] Another of Erasmus's views which runs directly counter to contemporary practice. Marriage alliances were the basis of the vast Habsburg Empire, and involved marriages between families separated by vast distances, where the couple shared no common language, customs, or affection.

[167] A comment closely related to Erasmus's own experience in the Low Countries. Maximilian acquired the Low Countries by his marriage to Mary, only daughter of the last duke. The people of the Low Countries remained hostile to him, but embraced their son, Philip the Fair (the addressee of Erasmus's *Panegyric*) enthusiastically as their native-born ruler. After his early death in 1506 the people of the Low Countries held out a similar hope for his son, Charles, and it is towards this hope that Erasmus's remarks about acceptable princes are directed.

Yet the common opinion is that such marriages are like iron chains of concord between states, although experience has shown that the greatest upheavals in human affairs arise from them; for example, it is alleged that some article in the marriage contract has been overlooked, or the bride is taken back because of some slight she is said to have received, or a prince changes his mind, renounces his first choice, and takes another to wife, or dissatisfaction arises in some other way. But what does this mean to the state? If marriage alliances between princes could guarantee peace in the world, I should be glad to see them all joined by a thousand marriage alliances. But did his marriage stop James King of Scots from invading England a few years ago?[168] It sometimes happens, too, that after many years of war's upheavals, after countless disasters, the quarrel is finally patched up by arranging a marriage, but only when both sides are already exhausted by their misfortunes.

The princes must set out to establish a perpetual peace among themselves and make common plans for it.[169] Even if a marriage brings about peace, it certainly cannot be perpetual. When one party dies, the chain of concord is broken. But if a peace were to be based on true principles, it would be stable and lasting. Someone will object that the begetting of children will perpetuate an alliance. But why then are wars most often fought between those who are the closest kin? No, it is the birth of children in particular which causes changes of ruler, when the right to rule is transferred from one place to another or when some territory is taken away from one state and given to another; the greatest upheavals usually arise from this sort of thing.

So these devices do not succeed in preventing wars but succeed only in making wars more frequent and more frightful. For if kingdoms are linked to one another by marriage, whenever one prince

Charles himself had been betrothed to Claude of France in 1501, then to Mary Tudor in 1507, and finally married Isabella of Portugal.

[168] In 1503, James IV of Scotland (1488–1513) married Margaret Tudor, daughter of King Henry VII of England. In the Anglo-French hostilities declared in 1513, however, he sided with the French against his brother-in-law Henry VIII, engaging with the English forces at the Battle of Flodden.

[169] Erasmus was one of those backing European diplomatic efforts at a 'perpetual peace', so that Christian Europe could consolidate her forces against the non-Christian power blocs (particularly the Ottomans) to the east.

has been offended he calls in all the rest, invoking the laws of kinship, so that for some trifling offence the best part of Christendom is immediately brought to arms, and one man's pique is mollified by an immense outpouring of Christian blood. I shall refrain, with good reason, from giving examples, to avoid offending anyone.[170]

To sum up, the fortunes of princes may be improved by alliances of this kind, but the fortunes of the people suffer and are diminished. The good prince, however, should consider that his own affairs are prospering only if this is compatible with the interests of the state. I shall pass over the fact that it is no way to treat one's daughters—to send them away, sometimes, to remote regions, to men entirely different in language, appearance, character, and thought, as if they were being sent into exile—when they would be happier to live in their own land, even with somewhat less pomp.

However, I can see that this custom is too well established for me to hope that it can be uprooted; but I thought it right to speak out, just in case things should turn out contrary to my expectations.[171]

10 *The business of princes in peacetime*

So the prince who is schooled in the doctrine of Christ and in the precepts of wisdom will hold nothing more dear than the happiness of his people: indeed, he will hold nothing else dear, and must both love and cherish them as one body with himself. He will devote all his thoughts, all his actions, all his energies to a single purpose, that of ruling the province entrusted to him in such a way that on the day of reckoning he will satisfy Christ and will leave a most honourable memory of himself among mortals.

Even if he is at home or in retreat the prince should imitate the worthy Scipio, who used to say that he was never less alone than when he was on his own and never less idle than when he had time to spare; for whenever he was free of public business, he would

---

[170] Charles's grandfather Maximilian was notorious for these kinds of dynastic power games.

[171] An uncharacteristically forthright statement by Erasmus of the distaste he and other moralists felt at the traffic in dynastic women which was used in the early sixteenth century (particularly by the Habsburgs) to strengthen their claim to territorial titles.

always be pondering some idea concerning the security or dignity of the state.[172] Let the prince imitate Virgil's Aeneas, whom the excellent poet often portrays turning over in his mind throughout the night, while others sleep, some way of helping his people.[173] Then there is this thought of Homer's, which should be inscribed on every wall of the palace, but most of all in the prince's heart; the sense of the verses, more or less, is: 'The man entrusted with a nation and its heavy business/Should not expect to enjoy a full night's sleep.'[174] Or, if he is out in public, he should always be contributing something to the common weal; in other words, he should never cease to be the prince.

It is better for the prince to be engaged in public duties than to spend his life hidden from sight. But whenever he goes out, he should take care that his face, his bearing, and above all his speech are such that they will set his people an example, bearing in mind that whatever he says or does will be seen by all and known to all. Wise men have criticised the custom of the Persian kings who spent their lives hidden away in their palaces. They sought the esteem of their subjects simply by never being seen in public, and by very rarely giving the people access to them. But if ever they did go out, it was to flaunt their barbaric arrogance and their immoderate wealth at the expense of the people. They used to fritter away the rest of their time in games or mad military adventures, as if the noble prince had nothing to do in time of peace, when in fact a whole crop of good works lies open to him, if only he thinks like a prince.

Some people today think that it is not very regal to be engaged in public duties, whereas in fact this is the only worthwhile occupation for a king. Similarly, some bishops consider that instructing the people, the one occupation worthy of a bishop, is the last of their duties, and for some strange reason they delegate to others the special duties of a bishop as unworthy of them and claim as their own all the most worldly affairs. But Mithridates, a king ennobled no less by his learning than by his empire, was not ashamed to dispense justice to his people from his own lips, with no interpreter;

---

[172] Cicero, *De officiis* 3.1, and Plutarch, *Moralia* 196 B. See also Erasmus, *Apophthegms*.
[173] Virgil, *Aeneid* 1.305.
[174] Homer, *Iliad* 2.24–5.

we read that he learned twenty-two languages thoroughly for the purpose.[175] Again, Philip of Macedon thought it no disgrace for a king to sit and listen to cases every day, and they say that his son Alexander the Great, though ambitious to the point of madness in other ways, had a custom of covering one ear with his hand while hearing cases, saying that he was keeping it free for the other party.[176]

The fact that some princes take no part in these duties can be explained by their perverse upbringing. As the old proverb says, every man likes to practise the skill he has learned but avoids those for which he knows he has no aptitude.[177] When a man has spent his early years among toadies and women, gambling, dancing, and hunting, corrupted first by perverse ideas and then by debauchery, how can he be expected afterwards to enjoy carrying out duties whose performance requires very careful consideration?

Homer says that a prince hasn't time to sleep all night;[178] but this kind have only one aim, to cheat the boredom of their lives by constantly finding new pleasures, as if the prince had absolutely nothing else to do. How can a prince, with his vast domains, find nothing to do, when the head of a family is kept busy enough by just one household?[179]

There are bad customs to be counteracted by good laws, corrupted laws to be amended and bad ones repealed, honest magistrates to be sought out and corrupt ones punished or restrained. The prince has to find ways to lighten the burden of the weakest classes, to rid his domain of robbery and crime with the least possible bloodshed, and to establish and secure lasting concord among his people. There are other tasks, less pressing but not unworthy of a prince, however great: he can inspect his cities, so long as his object is to see how they can be improved; he can fortify those which are vulnerable, enhance them with public buildings, such as bridges, colonnades, churches, embankments, and aqueducts, and

---

[175] Once again Erasmus cites the prince's competence in the vernacular languages of his territories with evident approval.

[176] Plutarch, *Life of Alexander* 42.2.

[177] *Adages* II.ii.82.

[178] Homer, *Iliad* 2.24–5.

[179] This is a good example of the way in which Erasmus's extended analogy of the prince as father of his people allows him to make it appear a simple and self-evident matter that the prince should behave according to everyday moral values.

clean up plague-spots, either by rebuilding or by draining swamps. He can divert rivers whose course is inconvenient, and let in or keep out the sea according to the needs of the town.[180] He can ensure that abandoned fields are tilled to increase the food supply, and he can direct that those producing useless crops be used differently, for example prohibiting vineyards where the wine is not worth making and where corn can be grown. There are a thousand similar tasks, whose supervision is an admirable job for the prince, and even a pleasant one for the good prince, so that he will never feel the need, bored by inactivity, to seek war or to waste the night gambling.

In his public acts, for example in public building or the games, or in receiving embassies if they involve the people's welfare, the prince should aim at a certain splendour, but without ostentation or extravagance. In his private life he will be more frugal and restrained, partly to avoid appearing to live at the public expense, and partly to avoid teaching his subjects extravagance, the father of many ills.

There was one error, I see, into which a great many of the Ancients fell—and I wish that there were none of our contemporaries doing the same—namely, that they directed all their efforts, not to improving the realm, but to increasing it; we can see that it often turned out that in striving to extend their power they lost even what they already had. Not without reason have Theopompus' words been much praised; he said that he was not interested in how large a kingdom he left to his sons, only in how much better and more secure it was.[181] It seems to me that that Laconic proverb 'You have drawn Sparta, now enhance it' might be inscribed on the arms of every prince.[182]

The good prince will be fully convinced that he can have no more worthwhile task than that of increasing the prosperity of the realm which fate gave him, and of enhancing it in every way. The conduct of General Epaminondas has been praised by learned men; when he was appointed, through envy, to a lowly office, one held in public

---

[180] Leonardo da Vinci was hired by Lodovico Sforza as engineer on a river-diverting project.

[181] Plutarch, *Moralia* 779 E; and see Erasmus, *Apophthegms*.

[182] See the long treatment of 'Spartam nactus es, hanc orna' which Erasmus added in the 1515 editions of his *Adages* (II.v.1).

contempt, he carried out its duties so well that it was regarded afterwards as one of the most honourable of positions and the greatest men vied for it; thus he showed that it is not the office that brings honour to the man, but the man to the office.

It follows that if, as we have tried to show, the prince gives particular attention to things which strengthen and ennoble the state, he will thereby drive out and keep out things which weaken the state. All this will be much assisted by the example, wisdom, and vigilance of the good prince, the integrity of magistrates and officials, the piety of priests, the choice of schoolmasters, just laws, and devotion to the pursuit of virtue. Therefore the good prince should devote all his attention to increasing and supporting these things. But the state is harmed by their opposites, which can be eliminated more easily if we try first to remove the roots and sources from which we know that they spring. The philosophy of the Christian prince involves dealing with things of this kind carefully and intelligently. It is entirely fitting for Christian princes to conspire, in a good sense, and to make common plans, against such things as these.

If the heavenly bodies are disturbed even for a short while or deflected from their true courses, it brings grave dangers to the world, as is obvious from eclipses of sun and moon. In the same way, if great princes stray from the path of honour, or sin through ambition, anger, or foolishness, they at once cause enormous trouble throughout the world. No eclipse ever afflicted mankind so gravely as the dispute between Pope Julius and King Louis of France, which we have witnessed and wept over only recently.[183]

11 On starting war

Although the prince will never make any decision hastily, he will never be more hesitant or more circumspect than in starting a war; other actions have their different disadvantages, but war always brings about the wreck of everything that is good, and the tide of war overflows with everything that is worst; what is more, there is no evil that persists so stubbornly. War breeds war; from a small

[183] Erasmus here refers to the hostilities between the militant Pope Julius II and Louis XII of France.

war a greater is born, from one, two; a war that begins as a game becomes bloody and serious; the plague of war, breaking out in one place, infects neighbours too and, indeed, even those far from the scene.[184]

The good prince will never start a war at all unless, after everything else has been tried, it cannot by any means be avoided. If we were all agreed on this, there would hardly ever be a war among men. In the end, if so pernicious a thing cannot be avoided, the prince's first concern should be to fight with the least possible harm to his subjects, at the lowest cost in Christian blood, and to end it as quickly as possible.

The truly Christian prince will first ponder how much difference there is between man, a creature born to peace and good will, and wild animals and beasts, born to pillage and war, and in addition how much difference there is between a man and a Christian. He should then consider how desirable, how honourable, how wholesome a thing is peace; on the other hand, how calamitous as well as wicked a thing is war, and how even the most just of wars brings with it a train of evils—if indeed any war can really be called just. Finally, putting aside all emotion, let him apply just a little reason to the problem by counting up the true cost of the war and deciding whether the object he seeks to achieve by it is worth that much, even if he were certain of victory, which does not always favour even the best of causes. Weigh up the anxieties, expense, dangers, the long and difficult preparations. You must call in a barbarian rabble, made up of all the worst scoundrels, and, if you want to be thought more of a man than the rival prince, you have to flatter and defer to these mercenaries, even after paying them, although there is no class of men more abject and indeed more damnable. Nothing is more precious to the good prince than that his people should be as virtuous as possible. But could there be a greater and more immediate threat to morality than war? The prince should pray for nothing more fervently than to see his subjects secure and prosperous in every way. But while he is learning to wage war, he is compelled to expose young men to all kinds of peril and to make

---

[184] Erasmus treats this topic at greater length in the 1515 adage, 'Dulce bellum inexpertis' (*Adages* IV.i.1). There are close parallels between the two treatments. Here again, his views coincide with those expressed by More in *Utopia* II.

countless orphans, widows, and childless old people, and to reduce countless others to beggary and misery, often in a single hour.

The world will have paid too high a price to make princes wise, if they insist on learning by experience how dreadful war is, so that as old men they can say: 'I never thought war could be so pernicious.' But, immortal God! what incalculable suffering has it cost the whole world to teach you that truism! One day the prince will realise that it was pointless to extend the frontiers of his kingdom and that what seemed at the outset to be a profitable enterprise has resulted in terrible loss to him; but before then many thousands of men have been either killed or maimed. These things would be better learnt from books, from the reminiscences of old men, or from the tribulations of neighbours. For years now this prince or that has been fighting for this or that realm: how much greater are their losses than their gains!

The good prince will arrange these matters so that they will be settled once and for all. A policy adopted on impulse will seem satisfactory for as long as the impulse has hold of you; a policy adopted after due consideration, and which satisfies you as a young man, will satisfy you as an old man too. This is never more relevant than when starting a war.

Plato calls it sedition, not war, when Greek fights Greek, and advises that, if this does occur, the war must be fought with the utmost restraint.[185] What word, then, do we think should be used when Christian draws the sword against Christian, since they are bound to one another by so many ties? What shall we say when the cruellest wars, prolonged for year after year, are fought on some slender pretext, some private quarrel, a foolish or immature ambition?

Some princes deceive themselves as follows: 'Some wars are entirely just, and I have just cause for starting one.' First, I will suspend judgment on whether any war is entirely just; but who is there who does not think his cause just? Amid so many shifts and changes in human affairs, amid the making and breaking of so many agreements and treaties, how could anyone not find a pretext, if any sort of pretext is enough to start a war?

It can be argued that papal laws do not condemn all war. Augustine too approves it somewhere.[186] Again, St Bernard praises some .

---

[185] Plato, *Republic* 5.470 C–D.
[186] Augustine, *City of God* 4.15 and 19.7.

soldiers. True enough, but Christ himself, and Peter, and Paul, always teach the opposite. Why does their authority carry less weight than that of Augustine or Bernard? Augustine does not disapprove of war in one or two passages, but the whole philosophy of Christ argues against war. Nowhere do the Apostles approve it, and as for those holy doctors who are alleged to have approved of war in one or two passages, how many passages are there where they condemn and curse it? Why do we gloss over all these and seize on the bits which support our wickedness? In fact, anyone who examines the matter more closely will find that none of them approves of the kind of war which is usually fought today.

Certain arts, such as astrology and what is called alchemy, were banned by law because they were too close to fraud and were generally managed by trickery, even if it were possible for a man to practise them honestly. This would be far more justifiable in the case of wars, even if some of them might be just—although with the world in its present state, I am not sure that any of that kind could be found, that is, wars not caused by ambition, anger, arrogance, lust, or greed. It often happens that the leaders of men, more extravagant than their private resources will allow, will take a chance to stir up war in order to boost their own finances, even by pillaging their own people. This is sometimes done by princes in collusion with one another, on some trumped-up pretext, in order to weaken the people and to strengthen their own position at the expense of the state. For these reasons the good Christian prince must be suspicious of all wars, however just.

Some, of course, will protest that they cannot give up their rights. First of all, these 'rights', if acquired by marriage, are largely the prince's private concern; how unjust it would be, while pursuing these rights, to inflict enormous damage on the people, and to pillage the whole kingdom, bringing it to the brink of disaster, while pursuing some small addition to his own possessions. Why should it affect the population as a whole when one prince offends another in some trifling matter, and a personal one at that, connected with a marriage or something similar?

The good prince uses the public interest as a yardstick in every field, otherwise he is no prince. He has not the same rights over men as over cattle. Government depends to a large extent on the consent of the people, which was what created kings in the first place. If some dispute arises between princes, why do they not take it to arbitration instead? There are plenty of bishops, abbots, scholars, plenty of grave magistrates whose verdict would settle the matter more satisfactorily than all this carnage, pillaging, and universal calamity.[187]

First of all, the Christian prince must be suspicious about his 'rights', and then, if they are established beyond doubt, he must ask himself whether they have to be vindicated to the great detriment of the whole world. Wise men prefer sometimes to lose a case rather than pursue it, because they see that it will cost less to do so. I believe that the emperor would prefer to give up rather than pursue the rights to the ancient monarchy which jurists have conferred on him in their writings.

But, people will say, if no one pursues his rights will anything be safe? Let the prince pursue his rights by all means, if it is to the state's advantage, so long as his rights do not cost his subjects too dear. After all, is anything ever safe nowadays when everyone pursues his rights to the letter? We see wars causing wars, wars following wars, and no limit or end to these upheavals. It is clear enough that nothing is achieved by these methods, and so other remedies should be tried. Even between the best of friends the relationship will not last long without some give and take. A husband often overlooks some fault in his wife to avoid disturbing their harmony. What can war produce except war? But consideration breeds consideration, and fairness, fairness.

The godly and merciful prince will also be influenced by seeing that the greatest part of all the great evils which every war entails falls on people unconnected with the war, who least deserve to suffer these calamities.

When the prince has made his calculations and reckoned up the total of all these woes (if indeed they could ever be reckoned up), then let him say to himself: 'Shall I alone be the cause of so much woe? Shall so much human blood, so many widows, so many grief-stricken households, so many childless old people, so many made undeservedly poor, the total ruin of morality, law, and religion: shall all this be laid at my door? Must I atone for all this before Christ?'

---

[187] As a direct consequence of Erasmus's view that the prince rules by consent, it follows that arbitration is a more appropriate solution to disputes about the prince's 'rights' than military hostilities.

A prince cannot revenge himself on his enemy without first opening hostilities against his own subjects. The people will have to be pillaged, the soldier (not for nothing called 'godless' by Virgil) will have to be called in. Citizens must be expelled from places where they have been accustomed to enjoy their property; citizens must be shut in in order to shut in the enemy. It happens all too often that we commit worse atrocities against our own citizens than against the enemy.

It is more difficult, and so more admirable, to build a fine city than to demolish one. We observe, however, that the most prosperous cities are built by private citizens, simple men, but are demolished by the wrath of princes. All too often we go to more trouble and expense to demolish a town than would be needed to build a new one, and we fight wars with such extravagance, at such expense, and with such enthusiasm and diligence, that peace could have been preserved for a tenth of all that.

The good prince should always seek the kind of glory that is bloodless and involves no harm to anyone. However well a war may turn out, there can be success only on one side, and on the other is ruin. Very often the victor too laments a victory bought too dearly.

If religion does not move us, or the misfortunes of the world, at least the honour of the Christian name should move us. What do we imagine the Turks and Saracens say about us, when they see that for hundreds of years the Christian princes have been utterly unable to agree among themselves? That peace never lasts, despite all the treaties? That there is no limit to the shedding of blood? And that there are fewer upheavals among the pagans than among those who preach perfect concord according to the doctrine of Christ?

How fleeting, how brief, how fragile is the life of a man, and how subject to misfortune, assailed already by a multitude of diseases and accidents, buildings which collapse, shipwrecks, earthquakes, lightning! We do not need to add war to our woes, and yet it causes more woe than all the others.

It used to be the task of preachers to root out all hostile feelings from the hearts of the common people. Nowadays the Englishman generally hates the Frenchman, for no better reason than that he is French. The Scot, simply because he is a Scot, hates the Englishman, the Italian hates the German, the Swabian the Swiss, and so on; province hates province, city hates city. Why do these ridiculous labels do more to separate us than the name of Christ, common to us all, can do to reconcile us?

Even if we allow that some wars are just, yet since we see that all mankind is plagued by this madness, it should be the role of wise priests to turn the minds of people and princes to other things. Nowadays we often see them as very firebrands of war. Bishops are not ashamed to frequent the camp; the cross is there, the body of Christ is there, the heavenly sacraments become mixed up in this worse than hellish business, and the symbols of perfect charity are brought into these bloody conflicts. Still more absurd, Christ is present in both camps, as if fighting against himself. It is not enough for war to be permitted between Christians; it must also be accorded the supreme honour.

If the teaching of Christ does not always and everywhere attack warfare, if my opponents can find one passage approving war, then let us fight as Christians. The Hebrews were allowed to engage in war, but with God's permission. On the other hand, our oracle, which re-echoes again and again in the pages of the Gospel, argues against war—and yet we make war with more wild enthusiasm than the Hebrews. David was beloved of God for his other virtues, and yet he was forbidden to build his temple for the simple reason that he was a man of blood, that is, a warrior—God chose the peaceful Solomon for this task.[188] If such things happened among the Jews, what will become of us Christians? They had only the shadow of Solomon, we have the true Solomon, Christ, the lover of peace, who reconciles all things in heaven and on earth.

However, I do not think, either, that war against the Turks should be hastily undertaken, remembering first of all that the kingdom of Christ was created, spread, and secured by very different means. Perhaps it should not be defended by other means than those which created and spread it. In addition we can see that wars of this kind have too frequently been made an excuse to fleece the Christian people—and then nothing else has been done. If it is done for the faith, this has been increased and enhanced by the suffering of martyrs, not by military force; if the battle is for power, wealth, and possessions, we must constantly consider whether such a course

---

[188] 1 Chronicles 22, 7–11; 2 Samuel 7, 12.

does not savour too little of Christianity. Indeed, judging by the people who fight this kind of war nowadays, it is more likely that we shall turn into Turks than that our efforts will make them into Christians. Let us first make sure that we are truly Christian ourselves and then, if it seems appropriate, let us attack the Turks.[189]

But I have written a great deal elsewhere on the evils of war, and this is not the place to repeat it.[190] I would merely exhort the princes who bear the name of Christian to set aside all trumped-up claims and spurious pretexts and apply themselves seriously and wholeheartedly to making an end of this long-standing and terrible mania among Christians for war, and to establishing peace and harmony among those who are united by so many common interests. To achieve this, they should exercise their talents, deploy their resources, draw up common plans, and stretch every sinew. It is in this way that those whose ambition it is to be considered great will prove their greatness. Anyone who can achieve this will have performed a far more dazzling deed than if he had subdued all Africa by arms. Nor should it prove too difficult to achieve, if each of us will cease to urge his own case, if we will set aside our personal feelings and work for the common cause, if our guide is Christ, not the world. At present, while each man looks out for himself, while popes and bishops are preoccupied with power and wealth, while princes are made reckless by ambition or anger, and while everyone else finds it to his advantage to defer to them, we are running headlong into the storm with folly as our guide. But if we acted with common purpose in our common affairs, even our private business

---

[189] Erasmus distances himself from contemporary arguments that Christendom ought to launch a consolidated assault on the Muslim Ottoman Empire in the name of Christ (an argument supported specifically by the Habsburgs, since the Ottomans were the only power bloc capable of posing a threat to their territories).

[190] Erasmus had already expressed outspoken anti-war views in his *Panegyric*, and in his 1515 *Adages*. His most extended treatment of the subject, *The Complaint of Peace*, was written, like *The Education of a Christian Prince*, shortly after his appointment as counsellor to Charles, and was published in 1516. It was written at the request of Jean le Sauvage, chancellor of Burgundy and Castile, a leading advocate of appeasement with France to secure lasting peace in the Netherlands. The dedication of *The Complaint of Peace*, addressed to Philip of Burgundy, bishop of Utrecht, stressed the urgency of reconciliation with France. 'In its political context, then, the *Complaint of Peace* is, like the *Panegyric* of 1504, a tract on behalf of that party in the Netherlands which favoured both peace with France and a peaceful solution of the conflict with Guelders' (Tracy, *Politics*, 56).

would prosper. At the moment, even the things we are fighting for are destroyed.

I have no doubt, most illustrious Prince, that you are of one mind with me, by your birth and by your upbringing at the hands of the best and most upright of men. For the rest, I pr   that Christ, perfect and supreme, will continue to favour your noble enterprises. He left a kingdom unstained by blood and he would have it remain unstained. He rejoices to be called the Prince of Peace; may he do the same for you, that your goodness and wisdom may at last give us relief from these insane wars. Even the memory of past troubles will commend peace to us, and the misfortunes of days gone by will make your good deeds doubly welcome.

Panegyric for Archduke Philip of Austria (excerpted text)

TO THE MOST REVEREND FATHER NICHOLAS RUISTRE, BISHOP OF ARRAS, FROM DESIDERIUS ERASMUS, GREETING[1]

For many reasons, most illustrious Bishop, I think it proper that the panegyric which I recently delivered to our prince on his return from Spain should reach men's hands under the auspices of your name above all others. First, because you give wholly disinterested support to letters, and always act as a kind of Maecenas or father to all learned men. Secondly, if this effort of mine can contribute anything worth while to enhancing the glory of our prince, no one cares more than you about the dignity of his position; or if it will serve rather to give him encouragement, that has always been your special interest, and from one Philip to another, from great-grandfather to great-grandson, it has been your constant concern to direct the minds of our rulers towards honourable purposes by your frank and wholesome counsel. Finally, I should like my speech to be recommended to readers of honest talents by the man through whom it previously won the approval of our prince: an approval he indeed gave evidence of himself by his eyes, his expression, and (as they say) his very brow, as well as by the generous remuneration which was a kind guarantee of his opinion.[2]

---

[1] CWE 27, 6–7; CWE 2, 79–85 [epp. 179, 180].
[2] Actually, it is not clear that Philip understood enough Latin to follow the oration closely as Erasmus delivered it.

Yet there were several reasons which suggested that I should make every effort not to publish: on the one hand I thought that I could call on only a limited amount of meagre talent, and on the other I was confronted by the formidable task of upholding the majesty of the noblest of princes in my oration, and it would be a serious disgrace to impair it through lack of ability. Certainly not everyone's brush can worthily reproduce the features of the godlike. And in addition to being unequal to the task for other reasons I was also debarred through shortage of time.

For indeed, not only had the idea entered my head too late, but I also knew nothing of the subject except what public rumour had conveyed to a man who was not particularly curious and was always muttering over his books. And so I hastily piled up a great jumbled mass of words, and then with the first strokes of the chisel I fashioned from them a sort of rough likeness of a panegyric. Afterwards I made a good many inquiries into the subject, but I could not gain much better information, through the negligence of some and the secretiveness of others; so that when there was a general demand for publication and I was unwilling to reweave the whole web, I strengthened it in several places. Consequently I fear that the experts will be all too ready to run their fingers over the speech and discover its unevenness and here and there its gaping seams.

Moreover, though eyes are the sole authorities for good narrative, I myself have not had the chance even of hearing any but a few, unconfirmed reports, so that this is an area which one must hurry over on tiptoe, so to speak. For to have written about a prince what was imperfectly known is a kind of sacrilege.

There was also the fact that my preference for frank speaking made me feel a certain distaste for all this kind of writing, to which Plato's phrase, 'the fourth subdivision of flattery' seems especially applicable, although it refers not so much to eulogy as to exhortation. But there is certainly no other method of correcting princes so effective as giving them an example of a good prince for a model, on the pretext of pronouncing a panegyric, provided that you bestow virtues and remove vices in such a way that it is clear that you are offering encouragement towards the one and deterrence from the other.[3] For doctors do not treat everyone in the same way,

---

[3] Erasmus repeated this justification for reprinting the *Panegyric* alongside *The Education of a Christian Prince* in 1516.

but in the way most appropriate to the individual case.[4] I could of course have protected myself with some such explanation, if I had not lighted on a prince who could be praised without any need to add fictitious details. On this last point I was fortunate, but those who will describe the same man in his later years will be more so.[5] May divine benevolence increasingly further his counsels on our behalf: that is my prayer. Farewell.

[While Erasmus was in Antwerp in 1504, seeing the *Panegyric* through the press, he wrote the following letter to Jean Desmarez (Paludanus), with whom Erasmus had been staying when he wrote it, and who, indeed, appears to have been responsible for getting Erasmus to write the piece. (Desmarez was public orator for the University of Louvain.)]

ERASMUS TO MASTER JEAN DESMAREZ
HIS LEARNED AND MOST KINDLY HOST, GREETINGS
Your letter, Jean Desmarez, the muses' delight and mine, tells me what I could easily guess even without a letter (so much more intent upon my reputation are you than I am myself), that you have for some time waited and thirsted to see what fortune, or guardian sprite perhaps, will attend my *Panegyric*, as it is born, so to speak, and comes into the daylight. The moment that first fresh page, still damp from the press, began to be shown about and passed from hand to hand, as novelties usually are, your friend Erasmus cocked up his ears (for you know how much delight he always took in that story about Apelles hiding behind his paintings), catching at every indication, not how many readers approved of it, since for me at least one single man's verdict would fully suffice to bolster my self-esteem, provided that man were like you or Valascus, but where it failed to win approval. For your encomiast is positively a nuisance unless his qualifications are exceptional, whereas the hostile critic, even if he is no expert, either reminds one of something one has

---

[4] Erasmus uses the extended analogy between a doctor and a prince in a variety of forms, throughout the *Panegyric* and *The Education of a Christian Prince*.

[5] Philip the Fair died in 1506. From Erasmus's point of view this meant, conveniently, that the extravagent expectations for the 'good prince' expressed in his 1504 oration were never proved excessive by the reality of his reign. When the *Panegyric* was republished in 1516 its praise for Philip was, above all, a compliment to his son Charles.

forgotten, or provokes one to defend what is well expressed, and so either improves the author's knowledge or at least increases his alertness; thus I am quite sure that I should in my right mind prefer a single mocking Momus to ten Polyhymnias.

But no need for words; I should say, on the whole, if it could appear to be said with as much modesty as truth, that there will be many more to find fault with the piece than to understand it. Now there are three kinds of fault-finders: the first kind (and I am not certain whether it excites my pity or derision more) consists of those who think themselves exceptionally well educated when in fact they are nothing of the kind; these men declare that I have made a slip on the very threshold of my *Panegyric* and run aground, as the saying goes, while I was still in the harbour, for they reckon as mistaken everything they fail to comprehend in it. Great God, what do they understand? So they perish like shrews given away by their squeaking; hard on the trail of other men's ignorance, they exhibit their own. But I would rather tell you the whole story in person. I am sure you will thoroughly enjoy it. At the same time I have a considerable respect for the two remaining classes of my attackers; they consist of those who naively and foolishly describe all this enthusiasm of mine for celebrating the prince as flattery, and those who have a smattering of letters and seem to find some things objectionable, or rather, perhaps a few things missing, in a work which is virtually unfinished as yet. Of these two criticisms the first has hurt me rather keenly because it seeks to cast an aspersion on my character; the other has less effect, because it assails only my intelligence and does not stain my reputation as well. Consequently I have to appease the latter critics as best I can, while the former must be answered more sharply.

First of all, those who believe panegyrics are nothing but flattery seem to be unaware of the purpose and aim of the extremely far-sighted men who invented this kind of composition, which consists in presenting princes with a pattern of goodness, in such a way as to reform bad rulers, improve the good, educate the boorish, reprove the erring, arouse the indolent, and cause even the hopelessly vicious to feel some inward stirrings of shame. Else can we believe that the great philosopher Callisthenes, who praised Alexander, or Lysias and Isocrates, or Pliny, and countless others, had any aim in writing works of this sort other than to exhort rulers to honourable actions under the cover of compliment? Do you really believe that one could present kings, born in the purple and brought up as they are, with the repellent teachings of Stoicism and the barking of the Cynics? Just to make them laugh, I suppose: or even to increase their irritation! How much easier it is to lead a generous spirit than to compel it, and how much better to improve matters by compliments rather than abuse. And what method of exhortation is more effective, or rather, what other method has in fact become habitual to men of wisdom, than to credit people with possessing already in large measure the attractive qualities they urge them to cultivate? Surely 'virtue, when praised, grows great; and boundless is the spur of fame'.

And did not the apostle Paul himself often use this device of correcting while praising (a sort of holy adulation)? Again, how could one reproach a wicked ruler for his cruelty more safely, yet more severely, than by proclaiming his mildness; or for his greed and violence and lust, than by celebrating his generosity, self-control, and chastity, 'that he may see fair virtue's face, and pine with grief that he has left her'.

But, it is objected, Augustine confesses that he uttered many falsehoods in singing the emperor's praises. How relevant it is that the writer was an implacable enemy of falsehood, we need not now discuss. Plato and the Stoics, at least, will permit the wise man to tell a lie in order to do good. Are we not right sometimes to inspire children to enthusiasm for goodness by means of false praise? Do not the best physicians tell their patients that they find their appearance and colour satisfactory, rather in order to make them so than because they are so? Besides, it is a sign of a generous disposition even to be slightly deluded in one's admiration for one's sovereign, and to forget the bounds of moderation in praising him to whom one's loyalty should be unbounded. It is, moreover, in the interest of the commonwealth that the subjects of any prince, even if he be not the best, should nevertheless have an exceedingly high regard for him; indeed, if the ruler should be undeserving of praise, it is for their benefit rather than his that the panegyric is written, for it is not offered merely to him who is its occasion, but also to the multitude in whose hearing it is pronounced. You must therefore adapt it largely to their ears, just as is done in sermons; and the resemblance of a panegyric to these is brought home to us by its

very name, which the Greek derives from a meeting of the multitude at large. For the same reason Quintilian is of the opinion that
no kind of oratory enjoys such freedom as panegyrics, and that in
them it is permissible to show off all the tricks and preciosities of
rhetoric in order to solicit the reader's attention. Finally, this kind
of thing is written for posterity and for the world; from this point
of view it does not matter much under whose name a pattern of the
good prince is publicly set forth, provided it is done cleverly, so
that it may appear to men of intelligence that you were not currying
favour but uttering a warning.

But those who press the charge of adulation apparently fail in the
first place to notice that it is not so much me as the prince that they
criticise; nor, in the second place, do they realise that the charge
recoils upon themselves as the greatest flatterers of all. Is this just
one more example of Hesiod's saying, 'potter with potter competes,
and joiner is jealous of joiner'? No: there is a huge gap between
their deplorable kind of adulation and this kind, which is not my
own but rather that of all scholars: for they praise even disgraceful
deeds and for their own advantage slavishly cozen the ears of fools,
whereas we offer to the gaze of the public what may be called the
lovely aspect of goodness, and that too in the name of the man to
whom virtue best beseems and under whose auspices it may most
easily be commended to the populace. And to any who complain
that the whole business of paying compliments is foolishness, I
might reply in Pliny's words that they only hold this view because
they themselves have ceased to deserve them. But let them be as
censorious as they like, only let us for our part write foolishness in
company with Ambrose and Jerome, who composed many personal
tributes of praise; for may I not have the same licence, in this popular and well-nigh theatrical kind of writing, as those holy men
enjoyed in their personal correspondence? I do believe that this
defence would seem creditable enough in the eyes of sensible critics,
even if I had written my *Panegyric* in praise of someone like Phalaris
or Sardanapalus or Heliogabalus; but as it is, in case I should be
suspected of insisting that any of the above considerations should
protect me from the charge of flattery, the prince I portrayed as
best I could was one who, for all his youth, in addition to his surely
unparalleled advantages of fortune, is already a shining example of
such great virtues, while every virtue may be looked for in him in

the future. From such a prince I should not so much expect gratitude for my devotion in writing his encomium, as stand in awe of
his displeasure, which God forbid: and this because of his own
extraordinary modesty, which makes any praise at all seem to him
excessive.

Again I shall be indicted by others, who are more familiar with
the glories of our prince than I, for representing all these glories as
smaller and fewer than they are. Whether I have done so I do not
know; but I have certainly attempted to arrange the scope and tenor
of the whole panegyric in such a way as to seem, in the eyes of
informed and attentive critics, to aim at anything but flattery:
indeed, as you know better almost than anyone, I have always been
so averse to this vice that I could not flatter anyone if I would, nor
would if I could. So I have no fear that that charge against my
character may be made good in the sight of those who, like yourself,
know your Erasmus 'inwardly and 'neath the skin'. Just as it is in
your power to witness to, or defend, my sincerity against them, so
too, as regards the slur on my abilities, none knows better than you,
since it was in your sight that the whole enterprise began and ended,
that three essential ingredients were missing: subject-matter, emotion, and time. The first of these is so important that without it you
have no means even of beginning your speech; for what could
Cicero himself achieve without a brief? The second has so much to
contribute that according to Quintilian it will make men full of
eloquence even without learning—and you know how hard you
found it to extract from me, how much difficulty I had in forcing
myself to undertake the task, how disinclined I was for it, in a word,
how little appetite I had for writing it. The third ingredient, again,
is of such consequence that not even the best of scholars can turn
out anything fully polished until it has been licked into shape by
'many a day, and many an erasure'. The prince had already reached
the frontiers of his realm before the idea occurred to you, and it
would have been tasteless to congratulate him on his return at a
time when the news of that event had turned stale, for what is out
of season is never to one's taste.

Accordingly what I may call a heap of words was raked together
in great haste. What else could I do, in my ignorance of the whole
subject? Now a speech without facts is like a body without bones.
The orator, however, is given certain facts; he does not fall short in

readiness to ask questions; but some persons answered me with details about splendid banquets and suchlike trifles, while others gave me reports too unreliable for me to venture to print them. But, if they had been as attentive to the prince's reputation in this respect as some are to their personal interest, I can see how dazzling the speech might be: however I should have to weave the whole fabric afresh; and it was still less encouraging to me that I had been deprived of all prospect of obtaining preliminary information. So I did the only thing I could and would do; I abandoned my former procedure and, as it were, stitched in new material at many places, extempore at that, in such a way that it should not clash with the rest of the fabric like badly sewn patches.

In this way I have undoubtedly made my *Panegyric* longer; whether better, I know not. It was also necessary sometimes to insert commonplaces as interludes and sometimes to add rather difficult digressions, and yet these themselves had sometimes to be altered to fit the subject matter of the prince's voyage. How enviable indeed, compared to my situation, was that of the younger Pliny! Not only was his a more fluent pen; not only had he a congenial emperor, who was already elderly and done with all his civil and military duties; even more important, most of the achievements he praised he had witnessed himself. For men give excellent accounts of what they know best; and we know nothing better than the events we have seen with our own eyes. For these reasons, then, Pliny dared to write a letter in which he stimulated the bored reader to observe with some care the figures of speech, the modes of transition, and the order. My duty is rather to ask my readers, who are lynx-eyed, to wink at many things. I can see for myself some gaps that still remain, some things far-fetched, some additions and disturbance of the natural order, some over-ripe language, and the absence of anything really finished or polished. Yet reasonably fair critics will not blame me for these drawbacks, but rather the disadvantages I have just described.

I have written all this at somewhat unusual length to you, my learned Desmarez (and to whom better than you?), since it seems to be your part above all to defend me against every accusation; not only because, through the kind of overflowing affection you entertain for me, you are generally as much affected by my fortunes as by your own, but also because it is on you that a great part of the blame, if reproof is what I deserve, or praise, if any praise is due to me, seems to fall. For it was you, if it was anyone, who urged me to undertake this task, reluctant and unwilling as I was, and you always spurred me tirelessly on to continue at it; you gave me the notion of offering it to our mighty prince, and helped me to do so; finally it was you again who refused to be satisfied until you had persuaded me to publish it. Even as the work progressed you made, among other suggestions, the following in particular, which I gladly accepted: that by an honourable mention in the speech I should as far as possible rescue from oblivion and obscurity the memory of that notable father in God, François de Busleyden, lord archbishop of Besançon, a man beyond all praise.[6] I have added a poem, cut from the same cloth; that is to say, extemporaneous, as you will easily perceive without any need for me to tell you so. Farewell, glory of literature; and be stout-hearted in defence of me, as you above all other men both can be and should.

Antwerp, at the printing house.

---

[6] François de Busleyden (died 1502) was the son of Philip the Good's secretary Giles de Busleyden. He was a gifted lawyer, and a member of the papal curia, who was tutor to Prince Philip, and subsequently one of Philip's foremost statesmen and counsellors. His political influence over Philip was very considerable: those like Henry of Bergen (one of Erasmus's early patrons) who fell out with Busleyden were quickly deprived of office and disgraced. He fell ill whilst accompanying Philip on the trip to Spain (begun in 1501) which Erasmus's *Panegyric* celebrates, and died near Toledo in August 1502.

Panegyric for Archduke Philip of Austria
to the most illustrious Prince Philip,
Archduke of Austria, Duke of Burgundy,
et cetera,
this panegyric of congratulation on his triumphal
departure
for Spain and most joyful return to his country,
by Desiderius Erasmus of Rotterdam, canon in
the order of
Saint Aurelius Augustine[7]

Like it or not, Philip, most fortunate of princes, you must accept my enthusiasm and take my presumption in good part, since I have undertaken the task of voicing the feelings of all your subjects, and congratulating you whom divine favour has happily returned to us. I have not done this simply so that you may thereby learn of the exceptional delight we all share (for of this you could convince yourself with your own eyes and ears, or easily judge it using your own powers of perception). In part I embarked on this so that I might broadcast as widely as possible the fame and publicity of this day to all peoples, which is the brightest and most auspicious ever known for our native land, now and in times to come (assuming I

---

[7] The *Panegyric* was delivered on 6 January 1504. It was first printed by Martens in Antwerp in February 1504, accompanied by the dedication to Ruistre, and the letter to Desmarez.

am able to say something worthy to be recorded for posterity).
Partly I did so because I was overwhelmed—I might almost say
intoxicated—with incredible joy, joy kindled passionately in the
hearts of one and all in unprecedented fashion by your longed-for
return, so that indeed I could not restrain myself from drawing
forth this incomparable happiness before your Highness, pouring it
out, and spreading it abroad.

So your Majesty will have to bear with my lack of moderation as
I bubble over with joy, for it is you who have provided so much
cause for it. It is difficult to keep silent in grief, as Cicero rightly
said. But it is the most difficult thing by far to refrain from speech
when you are carried away with happiness. For who has not learned
at some time from experience how hard it is to stifle in silence a
deep wound to the heart? Today we have learnt how much more
difficult it is to control boundless happiness, particularly when it is
the sweeter for coming at last in answer to anxious prayers; how
difficult to resist the tide of overflowing joy which the heart cannot
contain, to set a limit to rejoicing when there are no bounds to our
joy, or finally to speak with restraint when no speech can adequately
express our feelings.

[Erasmus describes the reluctance of the people of the Netherlands to see their young ruler leave on an extended journey, even
though they knew how important it was for him to visit his parents-
in-law in Spain, and have his Spanish titles formally bestowed on
him.]

Thus far I have spoken of your departure, now let me say a little
about your prolonged absence. Our concern and longing for you
had been increased by the longer than anticipated delay in your
return to us. For just as the jealous lover always fears the worst,
speed seems like slowness to someone filled with impatient longing.
Goodness, how long we found that year, how long seemed the
months we spent without you! For whom did that two-year period
(and it wasn't even quite that long) not feel like five or more? To
the impatient bridegroom time passes impossibly slowly and
unkindly; 'the year lags for wards held in check by their mother's
strict guardianship'.[8] So too the hours drag by when counted anxi-
ously by the parent awaiting a son's return on the allotted day.

---

[8] Horace, *Epistles* I.i.21–2.

There were even some who transferred to you the familiar Greek saying, and called you Callipedes,[9] not as a joke, as Tiberius Caesar[10] was once nicknamed when he lingered abroad, but sincerely, because of impatient longing for your return. At times, as if exhausted with longing, your native land showed its indignation at the way the time dragged, or at the business which delayed you, or even addressed you angrily with affectionate reproaches, demanding your presence in words such as these:

'When, I ask, will there be an end to your delaying, invincible prince, dearer to me than daylight? What has become of your concern for us? How could I have slipped out of your affections? Did I not bring you cheerfully into the world, cherish you gently in my bosom, and educate you assiduously until you reached maturity? I doubt if I shall ever see you again, unless you can tear yourself away before Spain has had its fill of you, before you have quenched the thirst of your father- and mother-in-law, or satisfied your sister's affection and your father's love. For if someone were to judge the length of time in terms of my desire for you, they would believe you already to have been away ten years and more.

'You do indeed owe much to Spain by marriage, but more to me on grounds of duty. Let me say this in justification: Spain, it is true, once gave your sister a husband, and more recently gave you a wife, but I gave you life. Spain crowned you, but I bore you. I admit I owe everything to you, but in return you owe yourself to me. That is a bold thing to say, but it is the truth. For I know I address my true prince, and not a tyrant.[11] Nor is it unknown to me that it was universally prophesied (and for a long time events have confirmed) that you are the one destined by heavenly decree to rule over many great empires. One land will claim you as king, another acknowledge you as emperor, yet another will adopt you under different titles. I pray this may be auspicious and fortunate for us both. But though I may have to give way to wealth and yield to splendour, and may indeed be inferior in all things, I shall still

---

[9] A Greek runner who made no progress.

[10] Suetonius, *Tiberius* 38.

[11] This is a recurrent theme in Erasmus's political writings, as also in political thought emanating from the Low Countries in general. A population is bound, according to Erasmus, to serve a prince born in direct line to the sovereign. A ruler who acquires a territory either by marriage or by conquest must obtain the *consent* of the population—otherwise he rules as a tyrant.

cling stubbornly to my one claim to fame: it was I alone who gave birth to my prince. The air elsewhere may be more congenial, but it was mine you first breathed. If another land may be more fruitful, nevertheless, this is the one which first took you in and nurtured you. If it is true that by some extraordinary means "native soil conquers us with its sweetness/And does not let us forget it", then it is I who am the keeper of your cradle.

'For this reason Jupiter (as mythology has it) delighted as much in his own Crete as in the heavens themselves, though Crete did not give him birth but only raised him. Ulysses was sumptuously entertained by Circe and Calypso, having travelled the world and seen so many opulent and delightful places, including the famous, marvellously fertile Egyptian delta. Yet he eagerly pursued his hazardous path back to rocky Ithaca, preferring to live any sort of simple life in his own country to a life with goddesses, feeding on nectar and ambrosia and never growing old (as Homer tells us). To the emperor Vespasian, the little house at Cosa where he was born was so dear to his heart that even when emperor he regularly visited the place which had given birth to such greatness. Nor did he allow anything to be changed, in case anything he had been accustomed to see should be lost; he preferred it to any other place, because there he had emitted his first cry. It was I who gave birth to you— not just a man and an ordinary person, but a most outstanding prince. Because I gave you birth, I claim you as my son; because I gave you suck, I claim you as my nursling; and because in you I gave birth to a prince, I can call on you as one who owes obedience.[12] So now at last I demand that you restore yourself to me, for you are owed to me on so many counts; in this way you will restore me to myself. Why have I claimed that I am fortunate, if others now enjoy my blessings? Please, please, I beg, let that generous heart of yours be touched at last by the personal affection of the one who reared you, or at least by the public concern expressed throughout your realm. As I learned to live without you, now finally allow me to enjoy your presence for a while.'

With this kind of complaining, induced by its impatient love, your country demanded that you should return. As for the powers

---

[12] Compare Erasmus's argument that birth implies mutual consent between ruler and ruled in *The Education of a Christian Prince*.

above, to whom it had entrusted you on your departure, what can I say concerning the passionate public and private prayers by means of which it begged them to restore your Highness? With what assiduous piety, offerings and prayers, it endeavoured to appease the divine powers, so that through their kindness this happiest of days might eventually dawn.

[Erasmus describes how the rulers of the territories through which Philip passed on his way to Spain (in particular the French king, Louis) competed in the lavishness of their welcome of him, and in the honours they heaped upon him.]

Now my speech is impatient to reach the destination towards which you were then hastening, that is, to Spain. It is easier to imply than to describe how much more lavish the celebrations were there, because there were so many reasons for rejoicing on both sides.[13] For indeed, that entire kingdom, the most widely extending and flourishing on earth today, as much for its wealth, as its nobility, its talent, and its splendour, laid all that at your feet to do honour to your arrival. And on top of all those riches, riches by means of which it triumphs over all other nations, Spain also surpassed everyone in its enthusiasm, as each man of rank on his own behalf, and all the people as one, did their utmost to pay you some tribute that would be worthy of your Highness, worthy of the memory of your sister, worthy of your love for your wife, worthy of the more than parental affection of the king and queen towards their son-in-law and daughter.

It would take too long even to enumerate the festive triumphs which you mounted for Spain, and which Spain in its turn put on for you. So many different deputations from the nobility met you in so many different locations, and in every district, city, and village there were scenes of public rejoicing. Each one of these individually was outstanding, and yet if they had all been rolled into one, they would have been outclassed by that special one on the seventh of May. That was the day on which Ferdinand, most magnificent of kings of this era (yet in nothing seeming to want to excel so much as in honouring you), sent on ahead large parties of leading members of the court and of prominent church men, and then between

---

[13] This was Philip's first official visit to Spain since his marriage to Ferdinand and Isabella's daughter, Juana, in October 1496.

the village of Balaguer and the town of Toledo met and embraced you and his beloved daughter. Then he led you through the thronged crowds of applauding noblemen and cheering people into the palace of Toledo. There the rejoicing began again when that formidable lady Isabella, one worthy to be counted amongst the great heroines of the past, received her longed-for son-in-law and her darling daughter with outstretched arms and kissed them, while tears of joy were shed on both sides.

You might have thought that nothing could be added to that day by way of joy and splendour, and yet it too was surpassed in every kind of magnificence by the fifteenth day following. Before a congregation formed of the cream of the Spanish nobility, you were installed and crowned with solemn ceremony as ruler of Castile, in a ceremony witnessed by every high dignitary of the ecclesiastical order, by the grace of God, in the presence of the king and queen surrounded by a vast crowd of civil officials and magistrates, in the cathedral of Toledo, which is dedicated to the Virgin. Those present swore allegiance to you with marvellous agreement and a previously unheard degree of enthusiasm. That day too was matched by the twenty-seventh of October, when with similar ceremonies you accepted the princedom of Aragon in the city of Saragossa.[14] Imagine what pleasure the Spanish people felt, accustomed as they are to the spectacle of virtue, when on beholding you they knew that their most fortunate kingdom would never lack the best of kings, and when they were able to call themselves doubly blessed because they were adopting a prince who excelled in every form of virtue, and because through you they could expect similar successors.

And indeed, everyone's hopes were confirmed and joy redoubled when your wife had a safe and happy delivery in the city, with the help of God, and laid in her parents' arms an exquisite little grandson, making you for the fourth time a father, and providing her native land with a precious pledge, left behind on behalf of both of

---

[14] The occasion for Erasmus's presenting his *Education of a Christian Prince* to Philip's son, Charles, was the latter's accession to the throne of Aragon on the death of his grandfather, Ferdinand. Strictly, Charles never graduated from 'prince of Castile' to its rightful ruler, since his mother, Juana, inherited the title from her mother Isabella (Juana was declared unfit to rule, and the title passed to Charles). Once again, Erasmus stresses the formal oath of allegiance, by means of which Philip's subjects consented to his rule.

you. What, pray, could be so timely and happy an answer to prayer? We can all imagine what immense joy filled your father-in-law's heart, who is as wise as he is devoted, and who is still vigorous and vital in his maturity, that he was able to see the one on whom the burden of his flourishing kingdom would safely rest, and already to enjoy with his own eyes a good portion of posterity in his children's children (as the poet says) and perhaps (God willing) he might be destined to see those too who will be born from them. In his old age he could justifiably consider himself fortunate for one of two reasons: either to be able to live to enjoy such a son-in-law yet longer, and the grandchildren who would be like their father, or to think he could now leave life with an easier mind because he saw he had fulfilled the last function of a good king once he had ensured that he could not be followed by an unworthy successor. The emperor Hadrian often used to say, when his adopted heir Commodus was seriously ill, 'We are leaning against a falling wall.' Indeed, all the most admired emperors thought nothing more important than to hand on the imperial succession to one like themselves or better. How then do you suppose your father-in-law felt, after a life from which no honour had been left out, and in which he had always taken first place, when he saw his merit brought full circle and completed by this supreme occasion—when you were at his side, no falling wall but a wall of bronze, well able to sustain not only the burden of empire but also its glory?

Such celebrations were as genuine as the real distress shown earlier, when an illness afflicted you for a few days at Balaguer and alarmed everyone. As soon as it was reported to the king, he hurried to your side in person, with only a small entourage, and without waiting on customary ceremony, in a state of fearful anxiety. That illness of yours could be considered to have been heaven-sent, if only because it revealed and released all the love and loyalty hidden deep in men's hearts. For even among princes the popular saying is true, that friends are acquired in good times but only tested in adversity, so that it would be worthwhile now and again for a man to meet with some misfortune, in order to discover for certain how loyal people really are to him. While times are good men's minds are not revealed, but bad luck sorts out false friends from true as readily as the alchemist's stone distinguishes pure gold from alloy. And so even the mishaps which befell you proved to be to your advantage, in enabling you to see now more clearly which people loved you on your own account rather than their own—though in your father-in-law's case no proof was needed of his affection for you. Nevertheless, fortune provided the occasion for demonstrating the extent of his love.

So, most illustrious Prince, you filled Spain to overflowing with joy first by your much-desired visit, then by regaining your health. Above all, because you were inaugurated as the new prince of Castile and Aragon—a king in the making. Then too because you had blessed a people already yours with a beautiful child born in their own land. Finally because you were fashioned, partly by nature and partly through your own efforts, to be one who would bring pleasure to all beholders in every way.[15]

[Philip's wife's parents found endless excuses to delay their departure, and the young couple finally left after a stay of a year and a half. Erasmus describes Philip's intervention to secure continuing peace between Spain and France on his way home, his emotional reunion in Savoy with his sister Margaret, and his dutiful visit to his father, the emperor Maximilian in Germany. He compares his travels to the wanderings of the mythical heroes of antiquity, and then to the historical heroes Alexander and Caesar. But whereas they brought war wherever they went, Philip brings peace, and wherever he goes he is welcomed with open arms. Some may think Erasmus is focusing too closely on Philip's good fortune, rather than his character. On account of his youth this is appropriate; time will reveal and confirm the full extent of his virtues. Philip has, indeed, been exceptionally fortunate (Erasmus enumerates some of his family successes, and compares other famous figures).]

It was your presence—yours alone—and your conversation which King Henry of England sought so eagerly that he did not hesitate to cross that channel which encircles his kingdom, and to enter, as it were, a new world, something which he had never done since he had come to the throne. In this situation there could be some uncertainty about which did you the greater honour: on the one hand

---

[15] Here are all the ingredients Erasmus requires in the Christian prince—a living example of the precepts in *The Education of a Christian Prince*. Philip (born in the Low Countries) has been appointed Prince of both Castile and Aragon by consent; his child is born within the territory, guaranteeing consensual succession; and nature and education have ensured that the designated prince is a good one.

that Henry (not a stupid man) should have decided to trust himself to the continent for a meeting of a few hours, leaving the safety of his island, though he well knew it was more dangerous for him to do so than for any Dionysius to leave Syracuse; or on the other your own openness and the integrity and personal commitment of your candid disposition, when you dispensed with your retinue and entrusted yourself, alone and unarmed, to British good faith.

The most distinguished king of France awaited your arrival with so much anticipation that he sent repeated invitations to you through his envoys, and was so happy to have you as his guest and so delighted to entertain you that he thought he was not so much honouring you as adding thereby to his own standing. The supremely wise and invincible king of Spain, who had added so many rich islands to his empire, had conquered so many cities, routed so many barbarians, enlarged his realm with so many victories and celebrated so many immortal triumphs, still thought that one thing was lacking to complete his happiness, namely that he had yet to see you—the one whom he intended to make partner in his wealth and power during his lifetime, and his heir after his death. And in order to achieve this, he sent embassies far in advance, using no less ingenuity and application in the project than he had expended on the greatest of his military campaigns. Each king chose to forget his resentment against the other rather than forgo the pleasure of seeing you, and neither bore a grudge against the other, because both were rivals in good will in their wish to embrace you.

Indeed, is there a noble prince anywhere who does not seek your friendship, aspire to be linked in marriage with you, or strive to be joined with you in some sort of relationship? This, indeed, Philip, is the finest indication of your good fortunes, in which you exceed all others, even the most fortunate, drawn (as they say) by white horses, nor are you inferior to any in anything else. For is there any mature man who could count as many outstanding honours and distinctions in a lifetime as have come to you in youth? So why should I proceed to compare your greatness with those whom antiquity placed in a brief list of happy men?

[Philip deserved his good fortune, because of his consistently virtuous conduct.]

You have so strongly conceived a kind of universal father's affection for your people that you are even inclined to spare the guilty, either if they are willing to come to their senses, or if you yourself permit something which is in breach of the law, but which can appear to have great force through your example. Besides, no virtue is more appropriate in princes nor more welcome to the people than kindness towards the deserving and forgiveness of wrongdoers. For everyone admires and praises the other virtues in so far as they concern himself, but kindness is applauded even by those who need nothing, and forgiveness is loved even by the wholly innocent. Other virtues are applauded as human, but this one is admired as something divine. For since the prince performs the function of a sort of divinity among mortals, and nothing is more disposed towards kindness or is more opposed to severity than a god (and indeed, as Pliny says, being a god means nothing else but one who aids a mortal), surely the greater the power anyone wields, the closer he ought to come to that image, and the nearer he approaches it, the more men will venerate him as if he were a god.

Again, cruelty in a king is so outrageous that no tyrant has ever been so rash as not to affect a kind of clemency. In spite of being much praised, however, very few rulers have demonstrated this quality without marring it with some fault attached to it. Maecenas' kindness of heart and abstention from bloodshed was marred by a damaging streak of weakness. Flavius Vespasian showed so much clemency that he is said to have wept even when handing down just punishment, but this virtue was obscured by his thirst for money. Julius Caesar's clemency was only simulated, Titus Vespasian affected it as part of his imperial power, and in many it concealed genuine cruelty. Lucius Cinna, along with many others, bears witness to the remarkable leniency of the emperor Augustus—Cinna led a conspiracy against Augustus, and was not only pardoned and allowed to go unpunished but was even received amongst the emperor's friends and called to the highest honours. The emperor Hadrian is recorded as having been so mild in disposition that he would never allow charges even of treason.[16] Yet the one stained the beginning and the other the end of his reign with bloodshed.

[16] *Crimen maiestatis.* Lewis and Short gives, 'high-treason; an offence against the majesty, sovereignty of the people'.

But in your own case, you win consistent praise for your compassion; nothing has ever been heard about you, or noted in your words, deeds, or gestures, which might indicate severity or harshness of temperament, so that it is quite clear that your own singular mildness is not artificially contrived or assumed temporarily, but is lasting and, indeed, innate and genuine. Nor are any of the other vices any more part of your make-up than is cruelty: not pride or arrogance, not over-hasty reaction to rumour, not hatred of truth and liberty, not love of deference and obsequiousness, nor any other such faults—faults which in general seem to be the natural concomitants of exalted status, or to arise from the fact that great princes are on the whole brought up too indulgently and treated too delicately. In one respect, though, they are not so fortunate: they rarely hear the truth. Everyone prefers to tell them what will please rather than what is for their good, and everyone believes it is more important to look after their own interests than the honour of the prince.

But you are influenced by the famous story of King Antiochus, who once got separated from the rest of his companions while he was out hunting, and at nightfall stopped at a cottage, alone and unrecognised, There, over supper, when Antiochus came up in conversation and those present spoke freely, he heard about his own shortcomings. At dawn his royal entourage arrived, greeted him, and produced his purple and diadem. Turning to the insignia he said: 'Last night for the first time since I put you on, I began to hear the truth.' In the same way Demetrius of Phalerum is said to have advised King Ptolemy to obtain books on how to rule the kingdom, and to turn to them for counsel and advice, because in books are be read the things that friends never dare to say.

You, though, do even better: you make it clear to your followers that nothing pleases your ears but what is truthful, frank, and sincere, and that nothing displeases you more than the anonymous whispers of malicious informers or the destructive insinuations of flatterers. For you know that there are two chief evils in court life, of which the most pernicious is false or unjust accusation, but by far the most dangerous is flattery. False accusation turns the prince against a few people, but flattery casts a spell over him entirely. So that Alexander Severus is justly praised, who so violently disliked this whole race of parasites that not only did he refuse ever to listen to them, but anyone who either bowed his head in saluting him or spoke seductive words of flattery was immediately sent away in disgrace; or if anyone was spared such punishment because of his rank, he was openly ridiculed. In this he proved himself greater than that other Alexander, the Great, whose greatness was undermined above all by the fact that he let himself be manipulated by flatterers. That emperor did deal with the related evil of those who make empty promises, though, executing them ('smoke-sellers', as they are called), by crucifixion and by suffocation by smoke. An emperor worthy of immortal dominion, indeed!

I would call on you to emulate him, I would propose this young man of your own age up to you for emulation, if you had not already embarked on that road of your own accord, whether this was instilled in you by some innate virtue or was grafted there by a nurturing education, which has often proved more effective than nature herself. For you do not measure your friends by their compliance but by their integrity, and you do not admit to your close circle of friends those who are agreeable, but rather those who are serious and prudent, respected for their learning and for their exemplary lives. Nor are you more careful in anything than in selecting those you esteem highly. You will certainly not be unaware of the absolute truth of a saying which Lampridius attributes to Marius Maximus, namely that a state is more fortunate, and probably safer, whose prince is wicked, than one in which the prince's friends are wicked, because one bad person can be corrected by several good ones, whereas many bad ones cannot by any means be triumphed over by one person, however good. But things can only be as good as is possible in that state in which the best of princes admits to his intimate circle only those who are just like himself, by whom he will neither be betrayed nor deceived. Such men will inspire him only with what is in his interests, true and contributing to his well-being, they will be too prudent to advise anything which he will subsequently regret, too scrupulous to put their own interests before those of their country, too eminent to be susceptible to flattery, and independent-spirited enough to dare to speak out.

But everything cannot fail to be for the best in a state where the best kind of prince admits to his close friendship only those most like himself, men who will neither sell him nor lead him astray, but who will instil into his ears only what is loyal, true and salutary, who will be too wise to counsel what must subsequently be regretted, too scrupulous to put their own advantages before their country's interests, too responsible to succumb to flattery, and too independent not to oppose vigorously any unworthy undertakings.

The sort of person it pleases your Highness to employ as counsellor can be amply documented by a single example (ignoring all others), François de Busleyden, archbishop of Besançon, of blessed memory, the regulator and fashioner of your childhood and your tutor in the liberal arts, a man born entirely for glory and greatness, framed for the service of his country, moulded to adorn a princely court; heaven-sent to defend, distinguish, and increase the greatness of your reign.[17] Clearly he was to you what Nestor was to Agamemnon, Parmenio to Philip of Macedon, Leonidas to Alexander, Cicero to Octavius, Phoenix to Achilles, Zopyrus to Darius. In Homer's *Iliad* Agamemnon wishes he had ten Nestors. Darius wanted as many Zopyruses as there are seeds in a pomegranate—he rated him so highly that he would rather have had him intact than have taken a hundred Babylons.

[Erasmus praises Busleyden lavishly. His loss must be almost intolerable to Philip, to whom, morally and intellectually, he owes to much. It is through him that Philip has been raised an outstandingly virtuous and benevolent ruler. He never forgets the oath he took to his people, he is bound by the laws of the land, and he does not levy burdensome taxes. In his personal life he is a worthy object of emulation.]

Up to now we have described Philip as peace-loving and fortunate—if only it might always be so, and we might never have to praise your planning in time of war. This is what we all hope, above all that chorus of learned and eloquent men who even now are earnestly making preparations to rescue your reputation from jealous oblivion. This chorus has always been peace's disciple; it flourishes only in happy times. It prefers solemn festivals to triumphs dripping with blood; it would rather celebrate your renown with joyful odes and panegyrics than with sad tragedies. It would rather serenade the name of an excellent prince for posterity on the delightful lyre, than on the fearful trumpet, and does not doubt that

---

[17] Erasmus's eulogy of François de Busleyden identifies his political affiliation. Busleyden belonged to the anti-war faction in Philip's entourage.

the former will be audible at just as great distance as the latter and will reverberate just as long. No one ought to fear that your moderation in time of peace will shine any less brightly in the future than the bravery of others in military affairs. For it is only the trappings of war which men admire, and not all men at that, nor even the most judicious, and deeds performed quietly, prudently, moderately, and justly are admired by all the best people, and indeed by everyone, and not just admired but loved. Furthermore, how little of the praise for a victory reaches the general, when every soldier claims a large share for himself, and fortune claims a yet larger one? Your praise rests on a firm foundation, and no one can detract from it. So that although greater fame may come from the pursuit of war, a better kind of fame derives from the art of peace.

What if praise for real determination, which some claim belongs to military affairs, actually shines forth more clearly in times of peace and prosperity than in the confusion of war? It does not matter if fewer people notice this, as long as they are better people. For in the first place, if the function of determination is to overcome difficulties with unbroken spirit, what part of each of our lives, I ask you, has not involved a struggle with the greatest difficulties? Cannot a resolute and enduring spirit be seen more clearly in prosperity than in adversity? Not to lose heart when things are hard does indeed show determination, but it shows far more not to become self-important when Fortune takes you to the top (for the simple reason that it happens less often) and not to indulge yourself in the smallest degree when Fortune is most indulgent.

In a storm, it takes more skill and strength to haul in your sails when a following wind is too strong than to avoid shipwreck when the winds are against you. Many people have resolutely stood up to the cruelty of Fortune, but very few have shown restraint when Fortune is kind. For in the former case the very difficulty of the situation seems almost to compel one to be virtuous, whereas in the latter good fortune encourages lack of self-control. Then again, defying dangers earns one praise, even though such praise is shared with a mere gladiator as well, and with the most despicable of pirates. Whereas mental self-control, sexual self-discipline, greed restrained, controlled temper, all earn a kind of praise which is reserved for the good and wise person. So that there are to be found in the annals of every nation large numbers of examples of men who participated in warfare with the utmost courage and with total disregard for their lives, but you find hardly anyone who, in times of national ease and happiness, governed the state with such restraint and prudence that their success did not make them abandon self-restraint nor deserving of someone's hatred or envy.

Furthermore, standard sources concede that a man may be wicked and yet be a good general and suitable to conduct a war, like the emperor Severus, about whom the senate pronounced that either he ought not to have been born or he ought not to die, since he was certainly of use to the state because of his diligence in military matters, yet he was a menace to the city because of his cruelty and all his other vices. Another example of this kind is Cornelius Rufinus, in whose support C. Fabricius said: 'I'd rather be robbed by a fellow-citizen than sold as a slave by the enemy.' But a man who is endowed with the kind of virtues which are performed in times of peace cannot be bad, not even as emperor. For wars are generally brought to an end by negotiations. The arts of peace are useful in every aspect of life; the arts of war are not. Therefore, whoever is a good prince is a good man; but, in general, the less good a man is, the better suited he is to war, so that praise for a prince ought not to be based on his military skills. Do we not observe that among the nations of men, as among wild animals, the fiercest and most savage are the fondest of fighting (for example, the Carians, the Scythians, and the British)? What about Hannibal? Was he not the greatest military leader because he was the worst and wickedest of men?

But the prince we really wish for—or rather the prince we have—must be completely and utterly virtuous. I will add one more to my heap of comparisons. It is a great deal more difficult to hold danger at a distance in quiet times than it is to counter danger in times of upheaval. But someone will say that it is a splendid thing, when the situation demands it, to defeat a foe by valour. Who denies that? But how much more splendid to act as if no one were your enemy. However outstanding it may be to beat back an enemy, it is surely a finer form of victory to stand aloof from him. We read that Antalcidas gave the following spirited reply to an Athenian who boasted about the vigour of his own city, and taunted the Lacedemonians with cowardice, saying: 'By Hercules, we have driven you out of Cephisus any number of times.' 'Indeed you have', countered

Antalcidas, 'but we have never yet had to drive you out of the Eurotas.'[18]

Antalcidas was justifiably boastful about this, but it would have been even more impressive if the Lacedemonians had subdued their enemy by benevolence, rather than by intimidation. For what can be more noble in a prince than to be so loved for his supreme humanity that not even those who have the ability to do so would wish to harm him, instead of being so feared for his martial skills that even those who are unable to hurt him would still like to do so? Would it not be a good deal safer to be held in such affection that there was not a single person who would not rather take up arms on your behalf than against you, instead of having many you were obliged to conquer? The Romans used to count up their triumphs and reckon up the provinces they had conquered. But at the same time they had to count how many nations and kings hated and despised their dominion. For anyone who dared challenge them felt contempt, and anyone forced into servitude felt hatred. It would have been most splendid for the Romans to have stopped their enemies taking up arms by intimidation, but most splendid of all if friendly feeling had bonded them to them.

You have experienced both states of affairs, which is something I esteem more highly than any victory; for outsiders all think highly of you on account of your many virtues, and especially for your reasonableness, clemency, and courtesy, so that none of them would wish to declare himself your enemy; and you are so dear to your own people that none of them would dare to do so. For no prince is more greatly feared by his enemies than one whose subjects do not fear him at all. You may ring yourself around with walls of adamant, surround yourself with a hundred ditches and ramparts, or go out like Milo, attended by a thousand strong men, still nothing protects your country better, and nothing guards your person more effectively, than your people's affection, earned honestly, as yours is earned.

Where is Alexander the Great now, who used to boast that he was called invincible? Where is Julius Caesar, who claimed that there was only one day on which he could have been vanquished?

[18] In other words, whilst the Athenians had had to make repeated efforts to recapture territory precariously held by them, the Spartans had always securely held the Eurotas, with no need for military engagement.

Do you not deserve the title of 'invincible' much more for maintaining peace than either of these two for winning their many victories? Undoubtedly the person who joins battle with his enemy comes closer to being defeated than the one who is so powerful that no one would dare to take him on, even if he wished, and who is so much liked that no one would wish to, even if he dared. And though it may be less bloody, that victory is certainly more spendid where the enemy yields voluntarily to you, than the one extracted with difficulty, through the hazards of war.

Finally, in addition to all this, though we may grant that glory in war is more illustrious, surely glory in peace is preferable? Imagine a situation in which a violent storm gives the helmsman the opportunity to demonstrate his skill—still, who would be so mad as not to prefer to make the passage across a calm sea? Granted that a serious illness gives a doctor the opportunity to demonstrate his competence, it is nonetheless not worth falling ill on that account. It may well be that a ruler can show his ability more clearly in difficult situations, but may the gods above grant that we may continue to love your moderation, justice, and benevolence in fortunate times, and may never have to admire your courage in times of uncertainty. Would not a doctor be inhuman if he wished plague upon the people to give himself greater prestige? Would not the people be utterly insane if they willed this upon themselves so that they could themselves boast of the prowess of the doctor? Who wouldn't think a sailor deranged who deliberately steered his ship on to the Symplegades or the Syrtes or into Charybdis' whirlpool the better to show off his navigational skills to the passengers? And would not they be more deranged than he if they deliberately endangered their lives to observe his prowess. Yet we may read of many rulers who liked nothing better than the outbreak of a war, for no better reason than so that they could increase their own renown.

What could be more cruel than this, what could come closer to the mentality of the most evil-minded villain? What could be more senseless than for the people to wish so much trouble on themselves so that they could glory in their belligerent leader? Let the gods above make our enemies think that way; we would rather, Philip, that you enjoyed a happy state of mind, than a turbulent one. Your kind of glory satisfies you, so it satisfies us. We utterly deplore that other kind of satisfaction. We prefer you as a peace-maker rather than as victor, and we prefer this to the extent that peace is in every way superior to war.

In peace the arts are pursued with enthusiasm, liberal studies flourish, respect for the law is held in high esteem, religious faith increases, wealth prospers, moral rectitude prevails.[19] In war all these collapse, are swept away, and become confused, and along with every kind of moral corruption there is no calamity which does not descend upon us. Sacred things are desecrated, divine worship is neglected, force takes the place of justice. For the laws are silent in the midst of war (as Cicero says), or if they say anything beneficial, they cannot be heard above the din of combat (as Marius put it elegantly). For what place could be found in such times for letters and the arts amid the noisy troops, the blare of trumpets and shrilling of bugles, the maddening thud of drums, the clanging of swords, and the fearful thunder of flying cannon-balls, which so upset wild animals, fish and birds that they leave their natural haunts and flee elsewhere? Which is why Homer in a number of places refers to 'the tumultous din of war'. The unfortunate old, meanwhile, are rapidly driven into intolerable grief, children are deprived of their fathers, wives have their husbands torn from them, arable land is laid waste, villages are deserted, shrines are torched, towns reduced to ruins, houses looted, and the fate of every honest man is put in the hands of the wickedest of criminals—and the largest part of these disasters inevitably falls upon those who are most innocent.

But enough of these kinds of misfortune. War brings yet more deadly evils (whose consequences even God himself could scarcely mend): adultery spreads, women forget their modesty, everywhere virgins are raped, young men, who have a natural tendency to vice, come to think that nothing matters and are swept into all kinds of crime, once order collapses and they can do so with impunity. All in all, if there was any sentiment of piety amongst men, it abandons us right away. The Furies burst out from the underworld, to confuse, overwhelm, and disorder the world by means of anger, frenzy, murder, bloodshed, and wickedness. Of course there are some vices even in times of peace, but they belong to comedy; whereas in war

---

[19] Erasmus's fundamental objection to war is its disruption of art and learning.

a procession of all tragedy's ills sweeps in indiscriminately, like a sea in flood, engulfing everything in disaster and wickedness. Besides, the kind of flagrant crimes which are committed in times of peace, and are punished by law with the utmost severity, are all spawned by war, and war's legacy. Arable land almost never gets rid of the salt deposit if it has ever been flooded by the sea. This, I say, this is the disgusting source from which spews out the dregs of criminality: robbers, rapists, pimps, marauders, pirates, bandits, assassins, poisoners, thieves, embezzlers, abortionists, agitators, traitors, profaners, perjurers, blasphemers, and also harlots, whores, and bawds. My voice would give out before I could finish itemising the monsters which war gives us, while in peace men can never forget the lessons they learned in the thick of war.

If only this harvest of so many ills were confined within the bounds of its own time and place, and would ripen and wither away with what generated it. As it is, the contagion spreads like the plague to the limits of the territory, and infects the entire region. Hence the lament of the most eloquent of poets: 'Alas for Mantua, which lies too close to Cremona!'

Then too the vices of war arise long before the actual war, and carry on long after it, so that the aftermath of war is almost more unpleasant than the war itself, and quite often even those who are victorious regret becoming involved. For at the first hint of a military campaign the dregs of humanity from all over the globe emerge from their hiding-places, and collect in dank puddles like bilge-water—men burdened by disgrace or debt, or in fear of the law because of their misdemeanours, or men conscious of their wickedness who think they cannot be safe in time of peace, or who have squandered their wealth, whom ignominious poverty has driven to the worse crime of robbing others.

Finally, there are those whose evil mind and evil spirit make them behave as if they had been born for wickedness, so that they would have dared to commit capital offences even if they had not thought their deeds would go unpunished, or that they might be rewarded for them. Wars are fought using these dregs of humanity—this filth has to be given a place in our cities and our homes, even though it would take a generation or more to purge their fetid presence from the moral world of your citizens. Just as nothing is so easily learned as depravity, so too nothing is so difficult to erase from our minds.

Add to this the fact that usually the greatest wars develop out of the smallest, and many wars from one. For it has never proved possible to terminate a single war. One war is linked to another, and drags along with it an interminable and inextricable chain of ills. These ills are so many that their number can barely be comprehended, they are so atrocious that even an utterly wicked man cannot make light of them. Yet these are the natural consequences of any war, however just. Furthermore, the grounds for starting a war are sometimes false, not infrequently contrived, and for the most part doubtful. Then the outcome of any battle is always uncertain, and finally, no victory is bloodless, and the fighting is always at the expense of the man who had least to gain by winning. So that I am led to declare boldly that the god-fearing prince will be far more astute to maintain peace, however unfair, than to embark on even the most advantageous war; for such a war will be preceded, accompanied, and followed by such an ocean of ills, so vast a swamp of wickedness, so black a plague of immorality.

For a Christian ruler, whose duty it is to be most merciful, not only believes that there is some divine presence who is just and mindful, but also knows that he will have to give that divinity an exact account of the spilling of even the tiniest drop of human blood; so that neither his entire realm nor even his own life ought to be so important to him that he would wish a single innocent man to die for him. Surely no such ruler will claim that he has some sort of entitlement (legitimate or otherwise) which would justify so many tears and bereavements, such painful grief and so much bloodshed, so many deaths, so many dangers and mutilations and (most damaging of all) such a pernicious spread of immorality? Will he not rather weigh up and balance impartially the profit he seeks against the deluge of ills he will unleash, and conclude that no war at all ought to be undertaken which can by any means be avoided?

We read that Julius Caesar, who had conducted warfare exhaustively in his desire for glory, in his final years became preoccupied with brooding upon the life he had finally to give up, tormented by a guilty conscience and by the ghosts of those whom he had killed passing incessantly before his eyes. Augustus, too, more than once considered stepping down as emperor. I imagine he hated the fact that the empire had been bought at the cost of so much human bloodshed. In the final stages of the conspiracy led by Lucius Cinna he exclaimed that not even life was so valuable that he was prepared to pay for his survival by the deaths of so many of his citizens. He also denied that any war ought to be undertaken unless it could be shown that there was greater hope of profit from it than fear of loss. Otherwise it was like fishing with a golden hook—if the hook should break off, its loss could not be made good by any catch. For this reason then, he said, no war should ever be undertaken unless absolutely necessary. In the *Lives of the Caesars* it is recorded that the pagan emperor Otho so hated civil war that he was filled with horror at the mere mention of it, and finally chose to take his own life, rather than risk the lives of so many men in his cause.

Oh what a noble spirit—if only our own Christian rulers shared it! For if they honestly reflect on what is indeed a fact, namely that the Christian world is one nation, the Christian church one family, the same race, the same city, and that we are all members of the same body, ruled by the same head in Christ Jesus, and informed by the same spirit, that we were all redeemed at the same price, equal heirs to a single inheritance, and that we all receive the same sacraments: then they must see that every war is a civil war—domestic and self-mutilating, even—if it is undertaken by Christians against Christians.

Of course it would once have been a matter of pride for the Spartans, the Athenians, and the Romans to have subdued as many nations as possible by military aggression, but they were heathens, capable, in my view, of sentiments worthy only of heathens. If that, indeed, since Plato and Aristotle in their works on the best kind of state both criticise the Spartan constitution which laid down warfare as their republic's ultimate good, when the greatest good for the state is peace, not victory. For peace is a good in itself, whereas victory does not belong to the category of goods which are intrinsic, but can only lead towards a good thing, and even then only if there is no alternative route available to peace. That state is best of all which does not extend its dominion by means of the arts of war, but which most closely resembles the celestial city. It contents itself with nothing so much as with leisure, peace, and concord. Therefore the Christian prince, who ought never to take his eyes off this model, should make this his principal source of fame: with all his might and exerting all his influence, to protect, honour and extend that which Christ, the prince of princes, left us as best and sweetest, namely, peace.

The best examples of the greatest spirits are those, in my view, who neither fear wars when they are unavoidable, nor provoke them when they can avoid doing so, and who are always ready and prepared to withstand them but never moved to undertake them unnecessarily. Wild animals prove their worth by attacking unprovoked; but men's greatness of spirit ought to be closely linked to admiration for innocence and prudence. To take up arms for any other reason than because peace cannot be maintained in any other way is not only to abandon virtuous goals, but to join forces with wickedness. If the prince's resolution is concentrated above all on protecting the lives and fortunes of citizens from the power of the enemy, why should we require you to carry out military duties, when up to now you have protected your people from harm far more effectively by means of your moderation, prudence, and justice?

We prefer the helmsman who uses his navigational skill to avoid dangerous rocks to one who risks sailing through them, and we regard the doctor who prevents sickness as superior to the one who uses medicine to mitigate it once it has developed. In the same way, we view a prince who uses wise counsel to ensure that war does not break out, as more distinguished than one skilled in military matters who directs hostilities with energy and expertise. Necessity is one thing, happiness quite another; remedies we are driven to are one thing, what we devoutly wish for another. So that the saying of King Agesilaus is justly praised, who, when he was asked by someone whether strength or justice was the greater virtue, replied, 'If we hold on to justice, then we will have no need of strength.'

For what more could we ask of the powers above as the outcome of any war, however successfully undertaken, than that your justice might continue among us undiminished? Even if we leave out of our calculations the ills which we have shown it to be the nature of war to bring with it, and weigh only the gains, which can often seem considerable, I still do not think that any of the most powerful rulers of history has achieved any more fortunate conditions through war than those which sensible citizens prefer in your own time with all the attendant advantages. If indeed there are two principal rewards of war: glory and extension of empire (for resources are never inexhaustible), then you have—completely peacefully—both increased your resources and moved forward the boundaries of empire; and you have earned greater fame by doing so than anyone else has achieved through the rigours of war. So that through your courtesy and good fortune you have won the applause of the world, which could never have been won by arms. Not even Rome, a city permanently at war, grew in renown as much in the generations of war it endured under her first seven kings as your realm has risen in prominence with no bloodshed and no carnage under your single rule (young though you are).

Moreover, there are clear indications that greater honours are to come. Already not only are you supreme in every kind of glory, but you excel in its magnitude, and its lasting renown. For if true glory is won by honourable means, as there has hardly ever been a war which the worst wickednesses have not contaminated, the only wise course of action to aspire to seems to be that from which justice, moderation, kindliness, tolerance, and other such virtues ensue. But perhaps that person was right who said that it was quite absurd to call the fame which is earned by a bad man, 'glory'. Nothing prevents a bad man being called a good soldier. But in general I cannot see how these two epithets can generally both be applied to the same person. So the leader who is by nature warlike is not glorious; but the leader who undertakes war only if forced to do so, who then carries it on for the good of the state rather than for himself, and finally who brings it to a close at the smallest cost in terms of his subjects' lives, to him is accorded the glory of war.[20]

[A peaceful prince can be glorious. Philip does not seem any the less manly and strong for being peaceable, nor does he detract from the shining reputation of his forebears. His example promises great things for his descendants.]

You understand that the good prince has a double duty: first, not just to look carefully after the legacy of glory inherited from his forebears, but to increase it further; and secondly, to pass on this fairest of possessions to his descendants. For it is not enough for

---

[20] This section of the *Panegyric* is one of a number of extended essays by Erasmus on the social destructiveness of war, the most well-known being his long adage, 'Dulce bellum inexpertis' ('War is sweet to those without experience of it').

the prince himself to be incapable of a bad action unless he has also ensured that a bad prince will never rule in his place. It is no easy matter, not just to keep up the reputation of men as illustrious as your forebears, but to surpass them; nevertheless, what gives you most cause for concern is what comes after you, because you know that it is more difficult to take responsibility for the conduct of others than for your own.

For this reason (for this topic ought not to be overlooked, since it has come up here) it is clear to us how much we owe to your sense of duty, for in nothing do you take more care than in your desire to make yourself wholly like your ancestors and your children just like yourself. And so you look after their upbringing as if you had produced them for the good of their country rather than for yourself. I consider them exceptionally fortunate to have been produced by parents like yourselves, not because you are distinguished or rich, but because you are perfectly in agreement in striving to ensure that your children are fashioned and instructed from earliest infancy, not for ambition and the din of success, but for true virtue. For children who are in every other way most fortunate are in nothing more unfortunate than when they are extremely well born, but extremely badly educated. For often such children are thoroughly spoilt, and brought up amongst swarms of flatterers who are entirely ignorant of virtuous practices, and whose manners and talk smack of nothing but material success; from people like this, they hear nothing serious or good for them, and they learn nothing from them except that a prince should behave arrogantly and impetuously.

But since so many things with which we are imbued in our earliest years mean so much to us, good God, how much care ought to be expended on educating those who nobody will dare to reprimand once they have grown up a little, and on whose behaviour the fortunes and morals of an entire population depends? You, therefore, entrust your own children only to conscientious and irreproachable nurses, and to wise and upright men, from whom they may absorb nothing through eye or ear which would be unworthy of their father; who, because they are exceptionally experienced, know how to imbue the unhardened clay of a childish mind with wholesome opinions, and dare to do so because they know it will please you; who wish to do so too because they are the best of men, and succeed because they work at it so diligently. For some time (I gather), you have been looking around to select a man tried and tested in personal behaviour and humane learning from amongst your many subjects, to whose loving care you can hand over these still tender nurslings so that he may educate them in those disciplines which are worthy of a prince.[21]

But let us return to the path from which for a short while we seem to have strayed. In order to show your children a perfect example of both military and civic virtue, no further example will be necessary than yourself, who have applied yourself to study with unequalled determination, nor will any praise be due to your ancestors which you may not be seen to have exemplified with your own virtues. Your paternal grandfather Frederick earned much praise for his moderation and wisdom. On the maternal side, your great-grandfather, whom you resemble in more than name, was conspicuous for the same peaceful virtues, without the military ones being absent. Your maternal grandfather Charles won most glowing renown, especially for his military skills. Your father Maximilian so excels in both kinds of virtue that it is difficult to decide whether he is more fierce in war or moderate in peace, more formidable to his enemies or deserving of love from his subjects, more audacious to his oponents or forgiving to those he has defeated. These almost divine talents of your father's, so wonderfully combining the emperor Frederick's wisdom and gentleness and Duke Charles' indomitable spirit, you yourself display so expressly and absolutely that you seem to be born either for peace or for war, and created so as simultaneously to be merciful and to be trained up to bravery.

Your gentleness, your justice, and your benevolence, we have long experienced these with great pleasure. But the experience of your hurling a thunderbolt with your right hand, and of the way you tower above your enemy, wielding sword and shield, that shall be left to those, whoever they may be, whose wicked deeds finally exhaust your exceptional patience and consideration. For none wage war more fiercely than those who engage in it with the greatest reluctance.

---

[21] This passage has been interpreted as a bid on Erasmus's part, on the occasion of the original delivery and then publication of the *Panegyric*, to secure the post of tutor to Philip's infant children for himself.

[There follows a final section of lavish praise for the name, reputation, and personal conduct of Philip. Erasmus describes the excitement and the festivities when the people learned of Philip's safe return. The panegyric ends with a further *laudatio* (speech of praise) for the exemplary young ruler delivered in the persona of his welcoming native land.]

The end of the panegyric delivered to the most illustrious prince Philip in the ducal palace of Brussels, in the presence of the most noble lord of Maigny, the high chancellor of Burgundy, and of the reverend father the bishop of Arras, before an audience etc. In the year after the birth of Christ one thousand five hundred and four, on the day of Epiphany.

Index

Index

Caligula (Gaius) 22, 26, 27
Callipedes 122
Callisthenes 114
Calypso 123
Carneades 56
Castile xvi, xix, 125, 127
Catholic Church ix, x, xv, xxi, 71
Charles VIII of France 95
Charybdis 136
Christ 13, 18, 29, 32, 34, 40, 42, 46, 60, 63, 78, 93, 98, 106, 107, 108, 109, 110
Cicero 117, 121, 132, 137
  Laws 62, 79
  Offices 62, 99
  Republic (lost) 62
Cinna, Lucius 129, 140
Circe 2, 41, 123
Claude of France 97
Claudius, Tiberius 27
Colet, John xiv
Commodus 35, 126
consent, government by viii, 17, 89, 105, 106, 122, 125, 126–7, 132
Cornelius Rufinus 134
counsellor 132
Council of Trent xvi
Cremona 138
Crete 123
Croesus 44, 50
Cyclops 12
cynicism 115
Cyrus x, 44, 50, 62

Darius 58, 62, 63, 132
Defence of Liberty against Tyrants xiv
Demetrius of Phalerum 60, 130
Desmarez, Jean (Paludanus) xiv, xvii, 113–19, 120
Diogenes the Cynic 2, 3, 55
Dionysius of Syracuse (tyrant) 25, 26, 52–3, 80, 128
Dionysius the Areopagite, *On the Ecclesiastical Hierarchy* 23
Domitian (tyrant) 26
Dorp, Martin xv
Duke Charles the Bold 77, 144

eloquence 63
Elyot, Sir Thomas xxiii
Emperor Ferdinand II xvi, xix
Emperor Frederick III 144

Emperor Maximilian xvi, xvii, xx, 1, 39, 74, 75, 98, 127, 144
England xiv, xv, xxi, xxii, 74, 97, 107, 127
Epaminondas 64, 101
Erasmus
  Adages xiii, xv, 10, 12, 23, 27, 29, 45, 49, 52, 74, 76, 83, 87, 88, 100, 101, 103, 109; 'Dulce bellum inexpertis' 103, 142; 'Scarabeus aquilam quaerit' 27, 34, 49; 'Spartam nactus es, hanc orna' 74, 77, 95, 101
  Apophthegms 20, 56, 60, 65, 99, 101
  Complaint of Peace xiii, 109
  De copia 63
  De ratione studii 10
  Jerome's *Letters* xv
  New Testament (*Novum instrumentum*) ix, xv, 59
  Panegyric 3, 7, 22, 34, 57, 67, 68, 96, 109, 114–45
  Praise of Folly xiv

Fabius Maximus 74
family/father of country 25, 26–7, 33–5, 59, 66, 100, 106, 127
Ferdinand of Aragon 124, 125, 127
flattery/flatterers xii, xvii, xix-xx, 2, 4, 8, 9, 11, 19, 21, 33, 43, 52–3, 54–65, 66, 90, 114–17, 130–2, 143
Flodden, Battle of 97
Florence xxiv, 40
foreign tours 68, 75
François I xvi, xxi
France 68, 77, 95, 97, 107, 109, 124, 128
Freiburg im Breisgau xv
friendship/friends xii, 94–5, 106, 130–1
Froben xv, xvi, xix, xxi, xxii, 8
Fugger bankers xvi, 76
Furies 137

Gelderland, Karl van Egmond, duke of 68
Germany 68, 95, 127
Gilles, Peter xvii
Greece/Greeks 96, 104, 122

Habsburgs vi, xiv, xvi, xxiii, 39, 65, 68, 74, 96, 98, 109
Hadrian 129
Hannibal 134
Helen of Troy 96

Index

Cambridge Texts in the History of Political Thought

Titles published in the series thus far

Aristotle *The Politics* and *The Constitution of Athens* (edited by Stephen Everson)

Arnold *Culture and Anarchy and other Writings* (edited by Stefan Collini)

Astell *Political Writings* (edited by Patricia Springborg)

Austin *The Province of Jurisprudence Determined* (edited by Wilfrid E. Rumble)

Bakunin *Statism and Anarchy* (edited by Marshall Shatz)

Baxter *A Holy Commonwealth* (edited by William Lamont)

Beccaria *On Crimes and Punishments and other Writings* (edited by Richard Bellamy)

Bentham *A Fragment on Government* (introduction by Ross Harrison)

Bernstein *The Preconditions of Socialism* (edited by Henry Tudor)

Bodin *On Sovereignty* (edited by Julian H. Franklin)

Bolingbroke *Political Writings* (edited by David Armitage)

Bossuet *Politics Drawn from the Very Words of Holy Scripture* (edited by Patrick Riley)

The British Idealists (edited by David Boucher)

Burke *Pre-Revolutionary Writings* (edited by Ian Harris)

Christine de Pizan *The Book of the Body Politic* (edited by Kate Langdon Forhan)

Cicero *On Duties* (edited by M. T. Griffin and E. M. Atkins)

Constant *Political Writings* (edited by Biancamaria Fontana)

Dante *Monarchy* (edited by Prue Shaw)

Diderot *Political Writings* (edited by John Hope Mason and Robert Wokler)

The Dutch Revolt (edited by Martin van Gelderen)

Early Greek Political Thought from Homer to the Sophists (edited by Michael Gagarin and Paul Woodruff)

The Early Political Writings of the German Romantics (edited by Frederick C. Beiser)

Erasmus *The Education of a Christian Prince* (edited by Lisa Jardine)

Ferguson *An Essay on the History of Civil Society* (edited by Fania Oz-Salzberger)

Filmer *Patriarcha and other Writings* (edited by Johann P. Sommerville)

Sir John Fortescue *On the Laws and Governance of England* (edited by Shelley Lockwood)